THE MINDFUL VOYAGER

SUSTAINABLE TRAVEL PRACTICES

DR. MINAKSHI BANSAL

DEDICATION

This book is dedicated to all the mindful voyagers who strive to explore the world responsibly, to those who believe that travel can be a force for good, and to the communities and ecosystems that welcome us with open arms. May your journeys be filled with wonder, discovery, and a deep appreciation for the beauty and diversity of our planet.

ϸϸϸ

Contents

Contents

Contents

Prayer

"Om Bhadram Karnebhih Shrinuyama Devah

Bhadram Pashyemakshabhiryajatrah

Sthirairangais Tushtuvamsastanubhih

Vyashema Devahitam Yadayuh

Svasti Na Indro Vriddhashravah

Svasti Nah Pusha Vishwavedah

Svasti Nastarkshyo Arishtanemih

Svasti No Brihaspatir Dadhatu

Om Shantih Shantih Shantih"

This mantra is a prayer for universal well-being, invoking the blessings of various deities for protection, health, and happiness. It emphasizes the importance of experiencing the auspicious through all senses and living a life aligned with divine purpose. The repetition of "Shantih" at the end signifies a deep desire for peace in the individual, the environment, and the universe at large. This mantra is often recited as a prayer for peace, prosperity, and the physical and spiritual well-being of all beings.

❧❧❧

About The Author

This book represents the culmination of extensive research and meticulous analysis, incorporating a diverse range of sources, including numerous books, scholarly studies, and personal experiences. Additionally, I have scoured various websites to gather relevant information and data essential for the compilation of this work. I have taken every precaution to ensure the accuracy of the information presented and have diligently cited all sources to acknowledge their contributions.

From her earliest days, Minakshi was distinguished by an insatiable appetite for reading. Her literary universe was inhabited by characters and narratives that spanned ethical tales, motivational and inspirational stories, and the mythic parables imbued with life lessons. This voracious reading habit was not merely for personal edification but was driven by a desire to distill and disseminate the essence of these narratives to foster the development of students and peers alike. She was particularly captivated by the lives and teachings of historical figures and spiritual leaders such as Adi Shankaracharya, Swami Vivekananda, Dr. APJ Abdul Kalam, Mahamana Pandit Madan Mohan Malviya, Mahatma Gandhi, Sardar Vallabhai Patel, and Vinoba Bhave, among others. Their philosophies and life stories fueled her ambition to embody their ideals of resilience, selflessness, and relentless pursuit of knowledge.

Dr. Minakshi's academic and practical engagement with psychology has been equally noteworthy. As a research scholar, her focus has been on exploring the intricate tapestry of the human psyche, aiming to unlock the potential for psychological well-being and societal harmony. Her scholarly work is complemented by her active involvement in social work, where she employs her academic insights to make tangible differences in the lives of the underprivileged. Her endeavours in social work are characterized by an innovative approach that combines traditional wisdom with contemporary psychological practices to address the multifaceted challenges faced by these communities.

Her artistic talents, another facet of her diverse capabilities, are not merely a personal passion but also serve as a medium through which she communicates and connects with others. Her art, rich in symbolism and emotional depth, reflects her philosophical inquiries and social concerns, offering viewers a glimpse into the breadth of her intellect and the depth of her compassion.

In addition to her contributions to the arts and social sciences, Dr. Minakshi has embraced the healing arts of Pranic Healing, mastering the techniques developed by Master Choa Kok Sui. This practice, which focuses on the manipulation of Prana or life energy to heal the body and aura, has been both a personal journey of discovery and a means through which she extends her healing touch to others. Her proficiency in Pranic Healing is complemented by her advocacy and teaching of various forms of meditation aimed at rejuvenation, personal betterment, and the cultivation of harmony within individuals and communities alike.

Dr. Minakshi's life is a narrative of relentless pursuit, not just of personal achievement but of the upliftment and empowerment of society at large. Her diverse interests and talents—spanning the arts, literature, psychology, and the healing practices—converge on a singular path of service. She embodies the spirit of the luminaries who inspired her, channelling their legacy through her actions and teachings. Through her books, art, and social initiatives, she continues to inspire a new generation to embark on their own journeys of self-discovery, resilience, and altruism.

Her commitment to social betterment, particularly her focus on uplifting underprivileged children, reflects a deep understanding of the transformative potential of education and personal development. By integrating her knowledge of psychology, her artistic sensibilities, and her healing practices, Dr. Bansal has developed a holistic approach to social work that addresses both the immediate needs and the long-term well-being of the communities she serves.

As an author, Dr. Minakshi's writings offer a blend of inspirational insights, practical wisdom, and reflective contemplations drawn from her extensive reading and life experiences. Her books serve as a guide for those seeking to navigate the complexities of life with grace, resilience, and purpose. Through her narratives, she extends an invitation to her readers to explore the depths of their own potential and to contribute meaningfully to the collective well-being of society.

In Dr. Minakshi Bansal, we find a remarkable synthesis of the artist, the scholar, the healer, and the social activist. Her life's work stands as a beacon of hope and a source of inspiration for individuals seeking to make a difference in the world. Her story is a compelling reminder of the power of individual action, rooted in compassion and driven by a profound commitment to the betterment of humanity. Dr. Minakshi's legacy is not just in the tangible outcomes of her efforts but in the enduring spirit of inquiry, empathy, and service that she embodies.

ppp

Preface

As I embarked on my own journey as a traveler, I was captivated by the world's wonders, from vibrant cultures to breathtaking landscapes. However, amidst the awe-inspiring experiences, I couldn't ignore the growing concern about the impact of travel on our planet and its inhabitants. This realization sparked a desire to explore a more conscious and responsible way to travel, one that aligned with my values of environmental stewardship and social responsibility.

My quest for sustainable travel practices led me down a path of discovery, research, and personal reflection. I delved into the complexities of the tourism industry, exploring its environmental and social impacts, as well as the emerging trends and initiatives that promote a more sustainable approach.

I interviewed experts, engaged with local communities, and immersed myself in diverse cultures, seeking insights and inspiration for responsible travel.

Through this journey, I discovered that sustainable travel is not just about minimizing our negative impact; it's about creating a positive one.

It's about respecting the environment, supporting local communities, preserving cultural heritage, and fostering a deeper connection with the places we visit. It's about recognizing that our choices as travelers have consequences, and that we have the power to make a difference through our actions.

This book is a culmination of my journey, a guide for those who seek to explore the world in a more mindful and responsible way. It's a collection of insights, tips, and stories that aim to inspire and empower travelers to embrace sustainable practices, reduce their environmental footprint, and contribute to the well-being of the communities they encounter. It's a testament to the belief that travel can be a force for good, a catalyst for positive change in the world.

In the pages that follow, you will find a comprehensive exploration of various sustainable travel practices. We will delve into the art of packing light, the importance of choosing eco-conscious accommodations, the joys of eating local, the allure of slow travel, and the significance of reducing waste.

We will explore the power of choosing low-impact transportation, the importance of supporting local economies, the responsibility of conserving water, and the necessity of reducing energy consumption. We will discuss the importance of respecting wildlife and ecosystems, the role of carbon offsetting, the value of educating ourselves about our destinations, and the joy of volunteering and giving back.

My hope is that this book will inspire you to become a mindful voyager, a traveler who not only seeks personal enrichment but also contributes to the well-being of the planet and its inhabitants.

Dr. Minakshi Bansal
Social Activist
Ahmedabad, Gujarat, Bharat

ppp

ONE

PACKING LIGHT: THE ART OF MINIMALIST TRAVEL

Embarking on a journey, whether a weekend getaway or a multi-week expedition, is an opportunity to explore new landscapes, cultures, and experiences. But the process of packing can often become a stressful endeavor, as we grapple with decisions about what to bring and what to leave behind. The mindful voyager understands that packing light is not merely a matter of convenience, but an integral part of sustainable travel practices. It's about minimizing our impact on the environment, supporting local communities, and embracing a more mindful approach to travel.

The essence of packing light lies in the art of minimalist travel. It's about curating a capsule wardrobe that can be mixed and matched to create a variety of outfits suitable for different occasions and climates. This involves prioritizing versatile pieces that can be dressed up or down, choosing fabrics that are lightweight and wrinkle-resistant, and packing only what is truly essential. By doing so, we not only reduce our luggage weight and make travel more manageable but also contribute to a lighter environmental footprint.

The benefits of packing light extend far beyond the practicalities of travel. It can enhance our overall travel experience, allowing us to move more freely and spontaneously, unburdened by excess baggage. It can also lead to a deeper connection with the places we visit, as we are less focused on material possessions and more open to new experiences and encounters. By embracing minimalist travel, we shift our focus from consumption to connection, fostering a more meaningful and enriching travel experience.

Choosing eco-conscious luggage is the first step towards packing light. Opt for durable, lightweight luggage made from recycled materials or sustainable sources. Consider investing in a carry-on suitcase to minimize your carbon footprint and avoid the hassle of checked baggage. A well-organized packing system can also make a significant difference. Utilize packing cubes or compression bags to maximize space and keep your belongings organized. This not only saves space but also helps prevent overpacking by visually compartmentalizing your items.

When it comes to clothing, prioritize quality over quantity. Choose versatile pieces that can be layered and combined to create different looks. Neutral colors and classic styles are often the most adaptable, allowing you to create outfits suitable for various occasions. Consider the climate and activities planned for your trip and pack accordingly. Avoid packing "just in case" items, as they often remain unused and contribute to unnecessary weight.

Footwear is another area where minimalist packing can make a difference. Opt for comfortable, versatile shoes that can be worn for both walking and dressier occasions. A pair of sturdy walking shoes or sandals, a pair of dressier shoes for evenings out, and perhaps a pair of flip-flops for the beach or pool should suffice for most trips. Remember, you can always do laundry on the go if needed.

Toiletries can also add unnecessary weight to your luggage. Opt for travel-sized containers and solid toiletries to minimize waste and save space. Consider using multi-purpose products, such as shampoo bars that can also be used as body wash, or a moisturizer that doubles as sunscreen. Remember, most hotels and accommodations provide basic toiletries, so you can often leave these items at home.

When packing electronics, be mindful of their weight and bulk. Consider whether you truly need to bring your laptop or tablet, or if your smartphone can suffice for most tasks. If you do bring electronics, be sure to pack the necessary chargers and adapters. Consider investing in a portable power bank to keep your devices charged on the go.

Packing light is not just about minimizing your luggage weight; it's also about minimizing your impact on the environment. Opt for reusable alternatives to single-use plastics, such as a reusable water bottle, coffee cup, and shopping bag. Bring a small reusable container for snacks or leftovers to avoid using disposable packaging. Consider packing a bamboo or metal straw to avoid plastic straws, and bring a set of reusable cutlery to avoid using disposable utensils.

By embracing minimalist travel and packing light, we not only reduce our environmental impact but also support local communities. We can do this by purchasing souvenirs and gifts from local artisans and markets, supporting local restaurants and cafes, and choosing accommodations that prioritize sustainability and social responsibility. By doing so, we contribute to the local economy and ensure that our travel dollars benefit the communities we visit.

Packing light is not just a practical approach to travel; it's a mindset that can enhance our overall travel experience. It allows us to be more present and mindful, to connect more deeply with the places we visit, and to prioritize experiences over material possessions. It's a way to travel more sustainably, responsibly, and meaningfully. As we embark on our journeys, let us remember that the most valuable souvenirs are not the ones we buy, but the ones we create through our experiences and encounters. Let us pack light, travel mindfully, and leave a positive impact on the world.

ᗡᗡᗡ

Packing light isn't just about convenience; it's a mindset. Embrace minimalism, prioritize experiences over possessions, and discover the freedom of traveling with only the essentials.

TWO

Choosing Eco-Conscious Accommodations: Supporting Sustainable Tourism

In the realm of sustainable travel, the choice of accommodation plays a pivotal role in minimizing our environmental footprint and contributing to the well-being of local communities. Eco-conscious accommodations prioritize practices that conserve resources, reduce waste, and support local economies. By choosing such establishments, travelers can actively participate in sustainable tourism and create a positive impact on the places they visit.

The concept of eco-conscious accommodations encompasses a wide range of practices that aim to minimize the environmental impact of the hospitality industry. This includes implementing energy-efficient technologies, such as solar panels and LED lighting, utilizing water-saving fixtures, and adopting waste reduction and recycling programs. These accommodations often source food locally, prioritize organic and fair-trade products, and support local businesses and communities. By choosing eco-conscious accommodations, travelers can actively contribute to these sustainable practices and promote a more responsible approach to tourism.

The benefits of choosing eco-conscious accommodations are manifold. They not only minimize our environmental impact but also enhance our travel experience by providing unique and authentic opportunities to connect with local cultures and environments. These accommodations often offer educational programs and activities that raise awareness about sustainability and local conservation efforts. They may also provide opportunities to interact with local communities, learn about traditional crafts and practices, and participate in eco-tourism activities that support local conservation efforts. By choosing eco-conscious accommodations, travelers can gain a deeper understanding of the places they visit and contribute to the preservation of their natural and cultural heritage.

When searching for eco-conscious accommodations, look for certifications and labels that indicate sustainable practices. There are various certifications available, such as LEED (Leadership in Energy and Environmental Design), Green Globe, and the Rainforest Alliance Certified seal. These certifications ensure that the accommodation meets specific environmental and social criteria, such as energy efficiency, water conservation, waste reduction, and fair labor practices. Additionally, many online platforms and travel guides specialize in eco-conscious accommodations, making it easier for travelers to find and book sustainable options.

Researching the accommodation's sustainability practices is crucial. Look for information on their website or inquire directly about their initiatives. Some key questions to ask include: How do they conserve water and energy? Do they have recycling and composting programs in place? Do they source food locally and support local businesses? Do they offer eco-friendly transportation options or encourage guests to use public transportation? Do they engage in any community development or conservation projects? By asking these questions, travelers can gain a better understanding of the accommodation's commitment to sustainability and make informed decisions about their choice of accommodation.

The size and type of accommodation can also impact its environmental footprint. Smaller, family-run establishments often have a lower environmental impact than large, chain hotels. They may have a smaller carbon footprint due to reduced energy consumption, less waste generation, and a more localized supply chain. Boutique hotels and bed and breakfasts often prioritize personalized service and unique experiences, which can enhance the overall travel experience. Additionally, staying in locally owned and operated accommodations supports the local economy and community.

The location of the accommodation is another important consideration. Choosing accommodations located in or near natural areas can provide opportunities to experience local ecosystems and biodiversity. This can involve staying in eco-lodges or wilderness camps that are designed to blend in with the surrounding environment and minimize their impact. These accommodations often offer guided nature walks, wildlife viewing opportunities, and other activities that allow guests to connect with nature. However, it's important to choose accommodations that prioritize responsible tourism practices and minimize their impact on the environment.

Sustainable tourism is about more than just choosing eco-conscious accommodations. It's about being mindful of our actions and choices throughout our travels. This includes minimizing our waste, conserving water and energy, respecting local cultures and traditions, and supporting local businesses and communities. It's about traveling in a way that benefits both the traveler and the destination, leaving a positive impact on the places we visit and the people we meet. By embracing sustainable tourism practices, we can contribute to a more responsible and equitable approach to travel that benefits both present and future generations.

In conclusion, choosing eco-conscious accommodations is a powerful way to support sustainable tourism and minimize our environmental footprint. By researching certifications, inquiring about sustainability practices, and considering the size, type, and location of accommodations, travelers can make informed decisions that align with their values and contribute to a more responsible approach to travel. Sustainable tourism is a journey, not a destination, and every choice we make along the way can make a difference. By choosing eco-conscious accommodations and embracing sustainable travel practices, we can create a positive impact on the world and ensure that our travels are not only enjoyable but also meaningful and responsible.

ᗡᗡᗡ

Sustainable accommodations are havens for conscious travelers. Seek out eco-certifications, inquire about their practices, and support establishments that prioritize environmental and social responsibility.

THREE

Eating Local: Embracing Culinary Adventures Responsibly

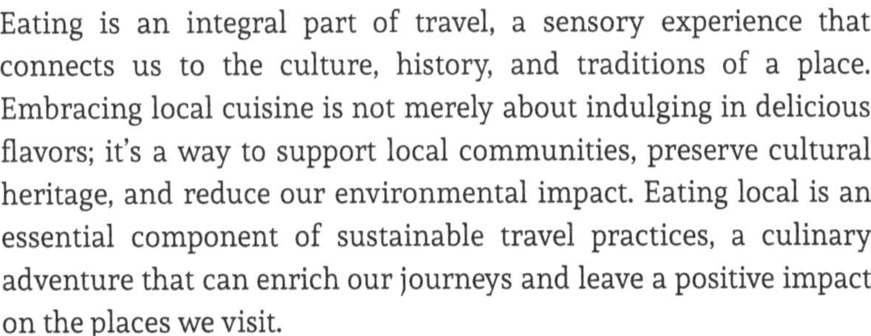

Eating is an integral part of travel, a sensory experience that connects us to the culture, history, and traditions of a place. Embracing local cuisine is not merely about indulging in delicious flavors; it's a way to support local communities, preserve cultural heritage, and reduce our environmental impact. Eating local is an essential component of sustainable travel practices, a culinary adventure that can enrich our journeys and leave a positive impact on the places we visit.

The concept of eating local encompasses more than just choosing restaurants that serve regional dishes. It's about seeking out fresh, seasonal ingredients sourced from local farmers and producers, supporting small, family-owned businesses, and exploring the diverse culinary traditions of a region. It's about understanding the connection between food and culture, and appreciating the unique flavors and ingredients that define a place. By embracing local cuisine, travelers can forge deeper connections with the communities they visit and contribute to the preservation of their culinary heritage.

Eating local has numerous benefits, both for the traveler and the destination. For the traveler, it offers an opportunity to savor authentic flavors and discover unique culinary traditions. It can lead to a deeper understanding of a place's history, culture, and environment. For the destination, it supports local economies, preserves cultural heritage, and promotes sustainable agriculture practices. It can also lead to a greater appreciation for local food and traditions, and encourage more sustainable and responsible tourism practices.

Seeking out farmers markets and local food vendors is a great way to experience the flavors of a region. These markets offer a wide variety of fresh, seasonal produce, local specialties, and artisanal products. They provide an opportunity to interact with local farmers and producers, learn about their farming practices, and discover unique ingredients. By purchasing directly from the source, travelers can support local economies and ensure that their food dollars go directly to the people who grow and produce it.

Exploring local restaurants and eateries is another way to embrace local cuisine. Look for establishments that prioritize local ingredients, traditional recipes, and sustainable practices. Ask locals for recommendations, or consult online guides and reviews that specialize in local food. Be adventurous and try dishes you may not be familiar with. You might be surprised by the new flavors and culinary combinations you discover. Remember, eating local is not just about the food itself; it's about the experience of discovering new tastes and traditions.

Cooking classes and food tours are a fun and educational way to delve deeper into the local cuisine. These experiences offer a hands-on approach to learning about local ingredients, traditional cooking techniques, and culinary customs. They often involve visits to local markets, farms, and producers, providing a deeper understanding of the connection between food and culture. By participating in these experiences, travelers can gain a new appreciation for the culinary traditions of a place and bring a piece of that culture home with them.

Responsible eating also involves being mindful of our choices and their impact on the environment. This includes choosing sustainable seafood options, reducing food waste, and minimizing our use of single-use plastics. It also means respecting local customs and traditions around food, such as avoiding eating endangered species or culturally sensitive ingredients. By making conscious choices about our food consumption, we can contribute to a more sustainable and responsible approach to travel.

In the context of sustainable travel, eating local is not just a trend; it's a conscious choice that can make a significant difference. It's about supporting local economies, preserving cultural heritage, and promoting sustainable agriculture practices. It's about appreciating the connection between food and culture, and understanding the impact of our choices on the environment. By embracing local cuisine and making responsible choices, we can create a more meaningful and sustainable travel experience that benefits both the traveler and the destination.

Eating local is a culinary adventure that goes beyond the plate. It's a journey of discovery, a way to connect with the people, culture, and environment of a place. It's about savoring authentic flavors, supporting local communities, and preserving culinary traditions. It's a conscious choice that can enrich our travels and leave a positive impact on the world. So, let us embrace the flavors of the world, one bite at a time, and embark on a culinary adventure that is both delicious and responsible.

ꝓꝓꝓ

Eating local is a culinary adventure that nourishes both body and soul. Savor the flavors of fresh, seasonal ingredients, support local farmers and producers, and immerse yourself in the rich tapestry of culinary traditions.

FOUR

SLOW TRAVEL: SAVORING THE JOURNEY, NOT JUST THE DESTINATION

In the fast-paced world of modern travel, where itineraries are often packed with back-to-back activities and destinations are rushed through in a whirlwind of sightseeing, the concept of slow travel emerges as a refreshing alternative. It's an invitation to savor the journey, to immerse oneself in the present moment, and to connect more deeply with the places and people encountered along the way. Slow travel is not merely a mode of transportation or a style of accommodation; it's a philosophy, a mindset that prioritizes quality over quantity, connection over consumption, and experience over efficiency.

At its core, slow travel is about slowing down and embracing a more mindful approach to travel. It's about savoring the journey, not just the destination. It's about taking the time to explore a place in depth, to wander off the beaten path, to interact with locals, and to immerse oneself in the local culture. It's about choosing quality over quantity, focusing on fewer destinations and spending more time in each place. It's about traveling at a pace that allows for deeper connections and more meaningful experiences.

The benefits of slow travel are manifold. It can reduce stress and enhance well-being, as it allows travelers to unwind and disconnect from the pressures of daily life. It can foster a deeper understanding and appreciation of different cultures and ways of life, as it encourages meaningful interactions with locals and immersion in local traditions. It can also have a positive impact on the environment, as it often involves choosing less carbon-intensive modes of transportation and supporting local businesses and communities.

Slow travel can take many forms, depending on individual preferences and interests. It can involve spending several weeks or months in a single location, immersing oneself in the local culture and exploring the surrounding area at a leisurely pace. It can also involve traveling between destinations slowly, by train, bus, or bicycle, taking the time to appreciate the scenery and interact with fellow travelers. It can even involve incorporating slow travel principles into shorter trips, by choosing a few key activities or attractions and dedicating ample time to each, rather than trying to cram too much into a limited timeframe.

Choosing alternative modes of transportation is a key aspect of slow travel. Instead of rushing from one place to another by plane, consider traveling by train, bus, or bicycle. These modes of transportation not only have a lower environmental impact but also offer a more immersive travel experience. Train journeys allow you to relax and enjoy the scenery, while bus rides offer opportunities to interact with locals and observe daily life. Cycling allows you to explore at your own pace, stopping whenever you like to take in the sights or grab a bite to eat.

Staying in locally owned accommodations is another way to embrace slow travel. Instead of opting for large, impersonal chain hotels, choose guesthouses, bed and breakfasts, or homestays. These accommodations often offer a more authentic experience, allowing you to connect with local hosts and learn about their culture and traditions. They also contribute directly to the local economy, supporting small businesses and families.

Engaging with local communities is an essential part of slow travel. Take the time to interact with locals, learn about their customs and traditions, and try their cuisine. Participate in local festivals and events, visit local markets and shops, and support local artisans and producers. By doing so, you not only gain a deeper understanding of the place you're visiting but also contribute to the local economy and foster cross-cultural understanding.

Slow travel is not just about how you travel; it's also about how you experience a place. Instead of rushing through a checklist of tourist attractions, take the time to explore a place in depth. Wander through local neighborhoods, visit local museums and art galleries, attend cultural performances, and simply observe daily life. By immersing yourself in the local culture, you'll gain a richer and more meaningful understanding of the place you're visiting.

In a world that often values speed and efficiency above all else, slow travel offers a refreshing alternative. It's an invitation to slow down, to savor the journey, and to connect more deeply with the world around us. It's a way to travel more sustainably, responsibly, and meaningfully. By embracing slow travel principles, we can transform our journeys into enriching experiences that leave a lasting positive impact on both ourselves and the places we visit.

❧❧❧

Slow down, breathe deep, and let the journey unfold at its own pace. Embrace slow travel, where meaningful connections and authentic experiences blossom in the unhurried moments.

FIVE

REDUCING WASTE: MINIMIZING YOUR FOOTPRINT ON THE GO

Traveling is an enriching experience, broadening horizons and fostering connections with diverse cultures and landscapes. Yet, the convenience and thrill of exploration can often come at a cost to the environment. The accumulation of waste, particularly single-use plastics, poses a significant threat to ecosystems and communities worldwide. However, mindful travelers recognize their responsibility to minimize their footprint and embrace sustainable practices. Reducing waste on the go is not just an environmental imperative; it is a conscious choice that reflects respect for the planet and its inhabitants.

The concept of reducing waste encompasses a multifaceted approach that extends beyond simply recycling. It involves rethinking consumption patterns, opting for reusable alternatives, and minimizing the generation of waste at the source. By adopting a zero-waste mindset, travelers can significantly reduce their environmental impact and contribute to a cleaner, healthier planet. This approach involves making conscious choices about the products we use, the packaging we consume, and the way we dispose of waste while on the move.

The benefits of reducing waste are numerous and far-reaching. It conserves resources, reduces pollution, and protects ecosystems from the harmful effects of waste accumulation. By minimizing our consumption of single-use plastics, we can help reduce the amount of plastic waste that ends up in landfills, oceans, and waterways. This not only benefits the environment but also protects wildlife and human health. Furthermore, reducing waste can also save money, as it often involves investing in reusable products that can be used repeatedly, rather than purchasing disposable items that are quickly discarded.

One of the most effective ways to reduce waste while traveling is to pack reusable alternatives to single-use items. This includes carrying a reusable water bottle, coffee cup, shopping bag, and food containers. By using these items, travelers can avoid purchasing bottled water, disposable cups, and plastic bags, which are major contributors to waste. Additionally, packing reusable cutlery, straws, and napkins can further reduce waste and minimize the need for disposable items.

Choosing accommodations that prioritize sustainability is another important step in reducing waste. Look for hotels and guesthouses that have implemented recycling programs, composting initiatives, and water conservation measures. Some accommodations even offer refillable toiletries and encourage guests to reuse towels and linens, reducing the need for washing and conserving water and energy. By supporting such establishments, travelers can encourage more sustainable practices in the hospitality industry.

Eating local is a delicious and responsible way to reduce waste while traveling. By opting for locally sourced food, travelers can avoid packaged and processed foods that often come with excessive packaging. Visiting farmers markets and local eateries not only supports local economies but also reduces the carbon footprint associated with food transportation. Additionally, carrying a reusable food container allows travelers to pack leftovers or snacks, minimizing the need for disposable packaging.

Transportation choices can also impact waste generation. Opting for public transportation, walking, or cycling can significantly reduce the carbon footprint associated with travel. When renting a car, choose fuel-efficient models or consider electric or hybrid options. By choosing greener transportation options, travelers can minimize their impact on the environment and contribute to a cleaner, healthier planet.

Supporting local businesses and communities is another way to reduce waste and promote sustainability. By purchasing souvenirs and gifts from local artisans and markets, travelers can support traditional crafts and skills, reduce the demand for mass-produced items, and contribute to the local economy. Additionally, choosing tour operators and activities that prioritize environmental responsibility can further reduce waste and support sustainable tourism practices.

Reducing waste on the go is an ongoing process that involves continuous learning and adaptation. It requires a shift in mindset from convenience to consciousness, from disposability to reusability. By embracing a zero-waste philosophy, travelers can transform their journeys into opportunities to make a positive impact on the planet. It's about making small changes that add up to a big difference, choosing reusable over disposable, and supporting businesses and communities that prioritize sustainability.

In conclusion, reducing waste while traveling is not just an environmental imperative; it is a responsible choice that reflects respect for the planet and its inhabitants. By adopting a zero-waste mindset, packing reusable alternatives, choosing sustainable accommodations, eating local, opting for greener transportation options, and supporting local businesses, travelers can significantly reduce their footprint and contribute to a cleaner, healthier planet. It's a journey of awareness, education, and action, a journey that can transform our travels into a force for good.

ϸϸϸ

Every step towards reducing waste is a step towards a healthier planet. Choose reusable alternatives, refuse single-use plastics, and embrace a zero-waste mindset, even on the go.

Choosing Low-Impact Transportation: Opting for Greener Options

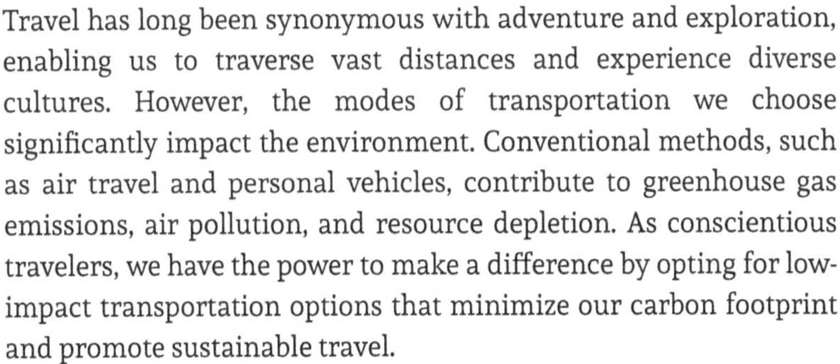

Travel has long been synonymous with adventure and exploration, enabling us to traverse vast distances and experience diverse cultures. However, the modes of transportation we choose significantly impact the environment. Conventional methods, such as air travel and personal vehicles, contribute to greenhouse gas emissions, air pollution, and resource depletion. As conscientious travelers, we have the power to make a difference by opting for low-impact transportation options that minimize our carbon footprint and promote sustainable travel.

Choosing low-impact transportation is a crucial step in mitigating the environmental impact of travel. By prioritizing greener options, we can reduce greenhouse gas emissions, conserve energy, and minimize pollution. Low-impact transportation refers to modes of travel that have a minimal impact on the environment, such as walking, cycling, public transportation, trains, and electric vehicles. These options offer a more sustainable alternative to conventional modes of transportation and contribute to a cleaner, healthier planet.

The benefits of choosing low-impact transportation extend beyond environmental conservation. They also contribute to personal well-being, community development, and economic sustainability. Walking and cycling promote physical activity, reduce stress, and improve mental health. Public transportation fosters social interaction, reduces traffic congestion, and improves air quality. Trains and electric vehicles offer comfortable and efficient travel experiences while minimizing emissions. By choosing low-impact transportation, we not only benefit the environment but also enhance our own well-being and contribute to the well-being of others.

When planning your travels, consider the various low-impact transportation options available. Walking and cycling are excellent choices for short distances or exploring local areas. They allow you to immerse yourself in the surroundings, discover hidden gems, and appreciate the details that may be missed when traveling at a faster pace. Public transportation, such as buses, trams, and subways, offers a convenient and affordable way to navigate cities and regions. Trains provide a comfortable and scenic way to travel longer distances, often connecting major cities and offering stunning views along the way. Electric vehicles, including cars, scooters, and bikes, offer a greener alternative to conventional vehicles, reducing emissions and promoting clean energy.

The choice of transportation mode depends on various factors, including distance, accessibility, budget, and personal preferences. For short distances within a city or town, walking or cycling may be the most convenient and eco-friendly options. For longer distances within a region or country, public transportation or trains can be excellent choices. If you are planning a road trip or need flexibility in your itinerary, consider renting an electric or hybrid vehicle. Researching and comparing different options allows you to make informed decisions that align with your sustainability goals.

Beyond choosing greener modes of transportation, there are additional steps you can take to minimize your environmental impact while traveling. Packing light can reduce fuel consumption and emissions associated with transporting luggage. Planning your itinerary efficiently can minimize unnecessary travel and optimize your transportation choices. Offsetting your carbon emissions through reputable organizations can further reduce your environmental impact. By combining these strategies, you can create a more sustainable and responsible travel experience.

Choosing low-impact transportation is not only an environmental imperative but also a cultural and social experience. It allows you to connect with local communities, interact with fellow travelers, and gain a deeper understanding of the places you visit. Walking or cycling through neighborhoods can provide a glimpse into daily life and cultural practices. Taking public transportation can introduce you to the locals and their routines. Train journeys can offer opportunities to engage in conversations with fellow passengers and learn about their stories. By embracing low-impact transportation, you open yourself up to a more enriching and immersive travel experience.

In conclusion, choosing low-impact transportation is a conscious choice that aligns with the principles of sustainable travel. By prioritizing greener options, such as walking, cycling, public transportation, trains, and electric vehicles, we can minimize our carbon footprint, conserve energy, and reduce pollution. Low-impact transportation not only benefits the environment but also enhances our own well-being, supports local communities, and promotes a more responsible and sustainable approach to travel. By making informed choices and adopting greener transportation options, we can create a positive impact on the planet and inspire others to do the same.

ᐅᐅᐅ

Let your transportation choices reflect your commitment to sustainability. Opt for walking, cycling, public transport, or electric vehicles, minimizing your carbon footprint and immersing yourself in the local rhythm.

SEVEN

SUPPORTING LOCAL ECONOMIES: PURCHASING FROM ARTISANS AND FARMERS

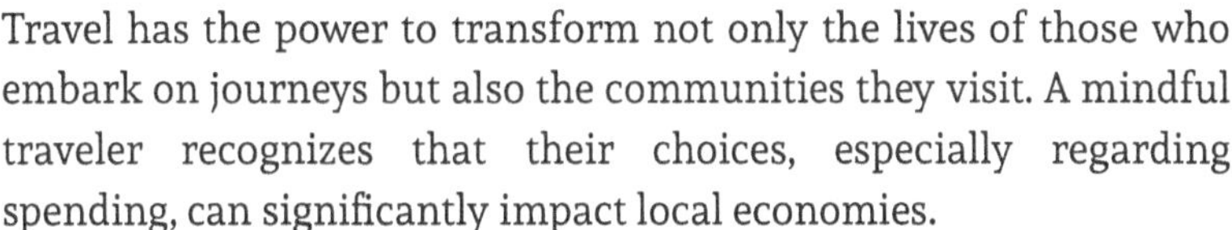

Travel has the power to transform not only the lives of those who embark on journeys but also the communities they visit. A mindful traveler recognizes that their choices, especially regarding spending, can significantly impact local economies.

By consciously choosing to support local artisans and farmers, travelers contribute to the economic well-being of communities, preserve cultural heritage, and foster sustainable development. It is an act of reciprocity, acknowledging the value of local craftsmanship and the importance of preserving traditional livelihoods.

Supporting local economies through purchasing from artisans and farmers is a multifaceted approach that extends beyond mere consumerism. It involves seeking out authentic products, understanding the stories behind their creation, and appreciating the cultural significance they hold. It is about forging connections with local producers, learning about their traditions and techniques, and contributing to the preservation of their craft.

By choosing to buy local, travelers not only acquire unique and meaningful souvenirs but also become part of a larger narrative of cultural exchange and economic empowerment.

The benefits of supporting local economies are numerous and far-reaching. It injects financial resources directly into communities, empowering artisans and farmers to sustain their livelihoods and invest in their businesses. It preserves cultural heritage by ensuring the continuity of traditional crafts and skills that might otherwise be lost to mass production and globalization.

It also promotes sustainable development by encouraging environmentally friendly practices and reducing the carbon footprint associated with long-distance transportation. By supporting local economies, travelers contribute to a more equitable and sustainable tourism model that benefits both visitors and hosts.

One of the most effective ways to support local economies is by purchasing directly from artisans and farmers. This can be done through various channels, such as visiting local markets, craft fairs, and workshops, or seeking out shops and galleries that showcase local products.

Many destinations also have cooperatives or associations that represent local producers, making it easier for travelers to find and purchase authentic products. By buying directly from the source, travelers can ensure that their money goes directly to the creators, rather than intermediaries or large corporations.

When purchasing from artisans and farmers, it is essential to prioritize quality and authenticity. Look for products that are handmade, unique, and reflect the local culture and traditions. Ask questions about the materials used, the production process, and the story behind the creation.

Many artisans and farmers are passionate about their work and are happy to share their knowledge and expertise. By engaging in conversations and learning about the product's origins, travelers can gain a deeper appreciation for its value and significance.

Supporting local economies also involves choosing accommodations and tour operators that prioritize local sourcing and partnerships. Many hotels and guesthouses now partner with local farmers and producers to source food, beverages, and other amenities.

Some tour operators offer experiences that focus on local culture and traditions, providing opportunities to interact with artisans and farmers and learn about their work. By choosing such establishments, travelers can ensure that their tourism dollars contribute to the local economy and support sustainable practices.

In the context of sustainable travel, supporting local economies is not just a trend but a conscious choice that aligns with the values of responsible tourism. It is about recognizing the interconnectedness of economic, social, and environmental well-being, and understanding the role that tourism can play in promoting sustainable development.

By choosing to buy local, travelers can contribute to the preservation of cultural heritage, the empowerment of local communities, and the protection of the environment.

Supporting local economies through purchasing from artisans and farmers is not merely a transaction; it is an act of cultural exchange and mutual respect. It is about valuing the skills, knowledge, and traditions of local producers and acknowledging their contribution to the richness and diversity of our world.

By choosing to buy local, we not only acquire unique and meaningful souvenirs but also become part of a larger movement that celebrates creativity, sustainability, and community empowerment. In the end, it is these connections and experiences that make travel truly enriching and transformative.

When you support local artisans and farmers, you invest in the heart and soul of a community. Seek out authentic crafts, savor local produce, and let your purchases empower those who create with passion and tradition.

EIGHT

Conserving Water: Being Mindful of Your Usage

Water, the essence of life, is a precious resource that sustains ecosystems, communities, and economies worldwide. Yet, its availability is not infinite, and its scarcity is a growing concern in many regions. As responsible travelers, we have a crucial role to play in conserving water, not just in our homes but also on our journeys. Being mindful of our water usage while traveling is a simple yet impactful way to contribute to sustainable tourism and ensure the availability of this vital resource for future generations.

Conserving water while traveling is not merely an act of environmental responsibility; it's an act of respect for local communities and ecosystems. In many destinations, water scarcity is a pressing issue, and local populations often face challenges in accessing clean and safe water. By being mindful of our water usage, we can help alleviate the strain on local water resources and ensure that everyone has access to this basic necessity. Additionally, conserving water can help protect fragile ecosystems and biodiversity, as many plant and animal species depend on water for their survival.

The benefits of conserving water are far-reaching and extend beyond the immediate context of travel. It helps preserve freshwater resources, reduces energy consumption associated with water treatment and distribution, and minimizes pollution caused by wastewater discharge. By conserving water, we not only contribute to a healthier environment but also promote sustainable development and improve the quality of life for communities worldwide.

One of the most effective ways to conserve water while traveling is to be mindful of our daily habits. This includes taking shorter showers, turning off the tap while brushing teeth or shaving, and reusing towels and linens. Many hotels and accommodations now have programs in place to encourage guests to conserve water, such as offering the option to decline daily housekeeping services or providing information on local water conservation efforts. By participating in these programs and adopting water-saving habits, travelers can significantly reduce their water consumption.

Choosing accommodations that prioritize water conservation is another important step. Look for hotels and guesthouses that have implemented water-saving technologies, such as low-flow toilets, showerheads, and faucets. Some accommodations also have rainwater harvesting systems, greywater recycling systems, and other innovative solutions to reduce their water footprint. By supporting such establishments, travelers can encourage more sustainable practices in the hospitality industry and contribute to water conservation efforts in the destinations they visit.

Eating local is another way to conserve water while traveling. The production of food, especially meat and dairy products, requires significant amounts of water. By choosing locally sourced food, travelers can reduce the demand for water-intensive products and support farmers who adopt sustainable agricultural practices. This can also help reduce the carbon footprint associated with food transportation, as local food travels shorter distances to reach consumers.

Transportation choices can also impact water consumption. Air travel and long-distance travel by car or bus can have a significant water footprint, as it involves the production and consumption of fuel. Opting for alternative modes of transportation, such as trains or public transportation, can be a more water-wise choice. When renting a car, consider choosing fuel-efficient models or exploring electric or hybrid options. By choosing greener transportation options, travelers can minimize their impact on water resources and reduce their carbon footprint.

Supporting local businesses and communities is another way to conserve water and promote sustainable tourism. Many local businesses, especially in water-scarce regions, have adopted water-saving practices and technologies. By patronizing these establishments, travelers can contribute to the local economy and encourage more sustainable practices. Additionally, participating in local conservation efforts, such as volunteering for beach cleanups or supporting organizations that work to protect water resources, can make a direct and lasting impact on water conservation.

Conserving water while traveling is not just about individual actions; it's about collective responsibility. By raising awareness about water scarcity and promoting water conservation practices, travelers can inspire others to adopt more sustainable behaviors. Sharing tips and experiences on social media, writing reviews on travel platforms, and engaging in conversations with fellow travelers can help spread the message of water conservation and create a ripple effect of positive change.

In conclusion, conserving water while traveling is a simple yet impactful way to contribute to sustainable tourism and protect a vital resource. By being mindful of our daily habits, choosing water-wise accommodations, eating local, opting for greener transportation options, and supporting local businesses, we can significantly reduce our water footprint and ensure the availability of clean water for future generations. It is a journey of awareness, education, and action, a journey that can transform our travels into a force for good. By conserving water, we not only protect the environment but also contribute to the well-being of communities and ecosystems worldwide.

❧❧❧

Water is life, a precious resource to be cherished and conserved. Be mindful of your usage, choose water-wise accommodations, and support initiatives that protect this vital element.

NINE

REDUCING ENERGY CONSUMPTION: UNPLUGGING AND CONSERVING

The modern world thrives on energy, powering our homes, businesses, and modes of transportation. Yet, the generation and consumption of energy often come with a significant environmental cost, contributing to greenhouse gas emissions, pollution, and resource depletion. As responsible travelers and global citizens, we have a crucial role to play in reducing energy consumption, not just in our daily lives but also while on the move. By adopting simple yet impactful practices, we can minimize our energy footprint, conserve resources, and contribute to a more sustainable future.

Reducing energy consumption while traveling is not merely an act of environmental stewardship; it's a conscious choice that aligns with the principles of sustainable tourism. It's about recognizing the interconnectedness of energy consumption, environmental impact, and social responsibility. By being mindful of our energy usage, we can help reduce greenhouse gas emissions, conserve resources, and support a cleaner, healthier planet. It's a small step that can make a big difference, both for the environment and for the communities we visit.

The benefits of reducing energy consumption are numerous and far-reaching. It helps mitigate climate change by reducing greenhouse gas emissions, which are a major contributor to global warming. It conserves valuable resources, such as fossil fuels and water, which are often used to generate electricity. It also improves air and water quality, as the burning of fossil fuels releases harmful pollutants into the environment. Additionally, reducing energy consumption can lead to cost savings, as it often involves using energy-efficient appliances and technologies that consume less power.

One of the simplest and most effective ways to reduce energy consumption while traveling is to unplug electronic devices and appliances when not in use. This includes unplugging phone chargers, laptop adapters, hair dryers, and other devices that consume standby power even when not actively used. Standby power, also known as vampire power, can account for a significant portion of household energy consumption. By unplugging devices when not in use, we can eliminate this unnecessary energy drain and reduce our overall energy consumption.

Another important aspect of reducing energy consumption is conserving electricity and water. Turning off lights and air conditioning when leaving a room, taking shorter showers, and using water-saving fixtures can significantly reduce energy and water usage. Choosing accommodations that prioritize energy efficiency, such as those with energy-saving appliances, LED lighting, and occupancy sensors, can further reduce our environmental impact. Additionally, being mindful of our transportation choices, opting for public transportation or walking instead of driving whenever possible, can help conserve energy and reduce emissions.

Reducing energy consumption also involves being aware of the energy sources used in the destinations we visit. Some regions rely heavily on fossil fuels for electricity generation, while others have invested in renewable energy sources, such as solar, wind, or hydropower. By choosing destinations that prioritize renewable energy, we can support the transition to a cleaner energy future and reduce our reliance on fossil fuels.

Supporting local businesses and communities is another way to reduce energy consumption and promote sustainability. Many local businesses have adopted energy-efficient practices, such as using energy-saving appliances, sourcing locally produced goods, and supporting renewable energy initiatives. By choosing to patronize these businesses, we can contribute to the local economy and encourage more sustainable practices in the tourism industry.

Reducing energy consumption while traveling is not just about individual actions; it's about collective responsibility. By raising awareness about energy conservation and promoting sustainable practices, travelers can inspire others to adopt more responsible behaviors. Sharing tips and experiences on social media, writing reviews on travel platforms, and engaging in conversations with fellow travelers can help spread the message of energy conservation and create a ripple effect of positive change.

In conclusion, reducing energy consumption while traveling is a crucial step towards a more sustainable future. By unplugging devices, conserving electricity and water, choosing energy-efficient accommodations, supporting local businesses, and being mindful of our energy sources, we can minimize our environmental impact and contribute to a cleaner, healthier planet. It's a journey of awareness, education, and action, a journey that can transform our travels into a force for good. By reducing energy consumption, we not only conserve resources but also support a more sustainable and equitable future for all.

❦❦❦

Unplug from excess and embrace mindful energy consumption. Turn off lights, conserve water, and choose accommodations that prioritize energy efficiency, leaving a lighter footprint on the planet.

TEN

RESPECTING WILDLIFE AND ECOSYSTEMS: OBSERVING FROM A DISTANCE

In the tapestry of our planet, wildlife and ecosystems play a crucial role in maintaining ecological balance and enriching our lives with their beauty and diversity. As travelers, we have the privilege of witnessing this natural splendor firsthand, but with this privilege comes a responsibility to respect and protect these delicate systems. Observing wildlife and ecosystems from a distance is not merely a matter of safety; it's a fundamental principle of ethical and sustainable travel, ensuring that our presence does not disrupt or harm the natural world.

Respecting wildlife and ecosystems entails a deep understanding of their intrinsic value and the interconnectedness of all living beings. It involves recognizing that we are guests in their habitats and that our actions can have profound consequences. Observing from a distance allows us to appreciate the natural behaviors and interactions of animals without causing them stress or altering their routines. It also minimizes our impact on fragile ecosystems, preventing soil erosion, vegetation trampling, and the spread of invasive species. By maintaining a respectful distance, we contribute to the preservation of these natural treasures for future generations to enjoy.

The benefits of observing wildlife and ecosystems from a distance are multifaceted and extend beyond environmental conservation. It can enhance our own travel experiences by fostering a deeper connection with nature and a greater appreciation for its wonders. It can also contribute to scientific research and conservation efforts, as our observations can provide valuable data on animal behavior, population dynamics, and habitat health. Furthermore, respecting wildlife and ecosystems aligns with the principles of ethical tourism, ensuring that our travels do not exploit or harm animals or the environment.

One of the fundamental principles of observing wildlife from a distance is to avoid approaching or disturbing animals in their natural habitats. This means refraining from feeding, touching, or chasing animals, as these actions can disrupt their natural behaviors and potentially put both the animal and the observer at risk. It's essential to use binoculars, spotting scopes, or telephoto lenses to observe animals from afar, allowing them to go about their daily lives undisturbed. It's also important to be mindful of noise levels, as loud noises can startle or frighten animals, leading to unnecessary stress or injury.

Respecting ecosystems involves being mindful of our impact on the environment. This includes staying on designated trails, avoiding trampling vegetation, and packing out all trash and waste. It also means being aware of sensitive habitats, such as nesting areas or breeding grounds, and avoiding disturbing these areas. When engaging in activities such as hiking, camping, or wildlife watching, it's essential to follow Leave No Trace principles, minimizing our impact and leaving the environment as we found it.

Choosing responsible tour operators and guides is another crucial aspect of respecting wildlife and ecosystems. Look for operators who prioritize ethical wildlife encounters, adhere to strict guidelines for animal welfare, and support local conservation efforts. Avoid tours that involve feeding or interacting with wild animals, as these activities can be harmful and disruptive. Instead, opt for tours that emphasize observation from a distance and provide educational information about the animals and their habitats.

Supporting conservation efforts is another way to respect wildlife and ecosystems. This can involve donating to organizations that work to protect endangered species and habitats, volunteering for conservation projects, or simply spreading awareness about the importance of wildlife conservation. By supporting conservation efforts, travelers can contribute to the long-term preservation of these natural treasures and ensure that future generations can experience their beauty and wonder.

In the context of sustainable travel, respecting wildlife and ecosystems is not just a matter of etiquette; it's a moral imperative. It's about recognizing the intrinsic value of all living beings and understanding our responsibility to protect them. It's about traveling in a way that minimizes our impact and leaves a positive legacy for future generations. By observing wildlife and ecosystems from a distance, we not only protect these delicate systems but also enrich our own travel experiences and contribute to a more sustainable and harmonious relationship with the natural world.

Observing wildlife and ecosystems from a distance is a journey of respect, appreciation, and wonder. It's a way to connect with nature on its own terms, to witness its beauty and complexity without causing harm. It's a conscious choice that aligns with the principles of ethical and sustainable travel, ensuring that our presence in the natural world is a positive one. By embracing this approach, we not only protect wildlife and ecosystems but also create more meaningful and transformative travel experiences for ourselves and for generations to come.

ppp

In the presence of wildlife, we are humbled observers. Maintain a respectful distance, avoid disturbance, and cherish the privilege of witnessing nature's delicate dance unfold.

ELEVEN

CARBON OFFSETTING: BALANCING YOUR ENVIRONMENTAL IMPACT

The modern traveler is increasingly aware of the environmental impact of their journeys, particularly the carbon emissions associated with air travel. As we explore the world, the undeniable truth is that our adventures contribute to the escalating climate crisis. Yet, amidst this growing concern, there emerges a concept that offers a glimmer of hope: carbon offsetting. It is a mechanism that allows individuals and businesses to compensate for their carbon emissions by investing in projects that reduce or remove an equivalent amount of greenhouse gases from the atmosphere. While not a panacea, carbon offsetting presents a viable way to balance our environmental impact and contribute to a more sustainable future.

Carbon offsetting is a complex yet essential concept in the realm of environmental responsibility. It recognizes that while we strive to reduce our carbon footprint, certain activities, such as air travel, inevitably result in emissions that cannot be entirely eliminated. To address this, carbon offsetting provides a means to neutralize these emissions by investing in projects that either prevent the release of greenhouse gases or remove them from the atmosphere. This can involve supporting renewable energy initiatives, reforestation projects, or energy efficiency programs, among others. By offsetting our carbon emissions, we can take responsibility for our environmental impact and contribute to a cleaner, healthier planet.

The rationale behind carbon offsetting lies in the understanding that greenhouse gases have a global impact. Regardless of where emissions occur, they contribute to the overall concentration of greenhouse gases in the atmosphere, leading to climate change. Therefore, by investing in projects that reduce or remove emissions elsewhere, we can effectively neutralize our own emissions and contribute to the global effort to combat climate change. Carbon offsetting also has the potential to support sustainable development projects in developing countries, creating a win-win situation for both the environment and local communities.

To effectively offset carbon emissions, it is essential to choose reputable and certified carbon offset providers. These providers invest in projects that meet rigorous standards for environmental integrity and social responsibility. They ensure that the projects they support are verified and monitored to ensure that they deliver the promised carbon reductions. Some popular carbon offset providers include Gold Standard, Verified Carbon Standard, and Climate Action Reserve. By choosing certified providers, travelers can be confident that their investments are making a real difference in reducing greenhouse gas emissions.

Carbon offsetting can be done in various ways, depending on

individual preferences and circumstances. Many airlines and travel companies now offer the option to offset the carbon emissions associated with flights or other travel activities. These programs typically calculate the emissions based on distance traveled and fuel consumption, and then offer the option to purchase offsets at a nominal fee. Alternatively, travelers can choose to offset their emissions independently through various online platforms and organizations that specialize in carbon offsetting. These platforms often provide a wider range of offset projects to choose from, allowing individuals to select projects that align with their values and interests.

The cost of carbon offsetting varies depending on the provider, the type of project, and the amount of emissions being offset. However, it is generally a relatively affordable way to take responsibility for our environmental impact. For example, offsetting a round-trip flight from New York to London might cost around $20-$50, depending on the provider and the project chosen. While this may seem like a small amount, the collective impact of many individuals offsetting their emissions can be significant.

It is important to note that carbon offsetting is not a substitute for reducing our carbon footprint. It should be seen as a complementary strategy, used in conjunction with efforts to reduce emissions at the source. This includes choosing more fuel-efficient modes of transportation, reducing energy consumption, and supporting renewable energy initiatives. By combining carbon offsetting with other sustainable practices, we can create a more comprehensive approach to addressing climate change.

Carbon offsetting has faced criticism from some quarters, with concerns raised about the effectiveness and transparency of certain offset projects. However, when done responsibly and through reputable providers, carbon offsetting can be a valuable tool in the fight against climate change. It is crucial to choose projects that are verified and monitored to ensure that they deliver the promised carbon reductions. Additionally, it is important to support projects that not only reduce emissions but also contribute to sustainable development and social well-being in local communities.

In conclusion, carbon offsetting offers a way to balance our environmental impact and contribute to a more sustainable future. By investing in projects that reduce or remove greenhouse gases from the atmosphere, we can neutralize our own emissions and support initiatives that address climate change. While not a perfect solution, carbon offsetting can be a valuable tool when used in conjunction with other sustainable practices. By choosing reputable providers, supporting verified projects, and continuing to reduce our carbon footprint, we can take responsibility for our environmental impact and contribute to a cleaner, healthier planet.

Carbon offsetting is a step towards balancing our environmental impact. Choose reputable providers, support impactful projects, and strive to reduce emissions in every aspect of your journey.

TWELVE
Educating Yourself: Learning About Your Destination's Culture and Environment

•♡•

In the tapestry of travel, knowledge weaves a vibrant thread, enriching our experiences and deepening our connection with the world. The mindful voyager understands that true exploration extends beyond the physical act of visiting a place; it encompasses a thirst for knowledge, a desire to understand the culture, history, and environment of our chosen destination. Educating ourselves about a place before and during our travels is not merely an intellectual pursuit; it is a transformative act that enhances our appreciation, fosters cultural sensitivity, and promotes responsible tourism.

The quest for knowledge begins long before we set foot on foreign soil. It starts with a curiosity about the destination, a desire to delve into its history, traditions, and natural wonders. Through books, documentaries, articles, and online resources, we can gain a preliminary understanding of the cultural nuances, social customs, and environmental challenges of a place. This pre-trip research lays the groundwork for a more informed and meaningful travel experience, allowing us to engage with the local culture and environment in a more respectful and appreciative manner.

Learning about a destination's culture involves understanding its history, traditions, language, art, music, and cuisine. It means delving into the stories, beliefs, and values that shape the lives of its people. This knowledge can be acquired through various channels, such as reading books and articles written by local authors, watching documentaries that showcase the cultural heritage of a place, and listening to music that reflects its unique sounds and rhythms. By immersing ourselves in the cultural tapestry of a destination, we open ourselves up to new perspectives, challenge our assumptions, and broaden our understanding of the world.

Language is a powerful tool for cultural exchange and understanding. Learning a few basic phrases in the local language can go a long way in building rapport with locals, showing respect for their culture, and enhancing our travel experience. It can also open doors to unique opportunities, such as conversing with local artisans, joining community gatherings, or navigating local markets with ease. Even a rudimentary understanding of the language can break down barriers and foster genuine connections with people from different backgrounds.

Art, music, and cuisine are vibrant expressions of a culture's identity and creativity. Visiting local museums, art galleries, and cultural centers can provide insights into the artistic traditions and historical narratives of a place. Attending traditional music or dance performances can offer a glimpse into the soul of a culture, while sampling local cuisine can tantalize our taste buds and reveal the culinary traditions that have been passed down through generations. By engaging with these artistic and culinary expressions, we gain a deeper appreciation for the cultural richness and diversity of our world.

Understanding a destination's environment is equally important for responsible travel. It involves learning about its unique ecosystems, biodiversity, and environmental challenges. This knowledge can be acquired through various sources, such as reading books and articles about the region's natural history, watching documentaries that showcase its landscapes and wildlife, and consulting online resources that provide information on local conservation efforts. By understanding the environmental context of a place, we can make informed decisions about our activities and choices, minimizing our impact and supporting sustainable tourism practices.

Respect for the environment is a cornerstone of responsible travel. It means treading lightly on the earth, minimizing our waste, conserving resources, and supporting initiatives that protect natural habitats and wildlife. It also means being mindful of our carbon footprint and choosing transportation options that have a lower environmental impact. By respecting the environment, we not only contribute to its preservation but also ensure that future generations can enjoy its beauty and wonder.

Engaging with local communities is an essential aspect of learning about a destination's culture and environment. It involves interacting with locals, listening to their stories, and learning from their perspectives. This can be done through various means, such as staying in locally owned accommodations, participating in community-based tourism initiatives, and volunteering for local projects. By engaging with local communities, we not only gain valuable insights into their lives and cultures but also contribute to their well-being and empowerment.

In the age of information, there are numerous resources available to help us educate ourselves about our destinations. Libraries, bookstores, and online platforms offer a wealth of information on various cultures and environments. Travel guides, documentaries, and blogs can provide valuable insights and recommendations. Additionally, many destinations have visitor centers, museums, and cultural institutions that offer educational programs and exhibits that showcase the unique aspects of their culture and environment. By utilizing these resources and engaging with local experts and communities, we can gain a deeper understanding of the places we visit and become more informed and responsible travelers.

In conclusion, educating ourselves about a destination's culture and environment is an integral part of the mindful voyager's journey. It is a transformative process that enriches our experiences, fosters cultural sensitivity, and promotes responsible tourism. By learning about the history, traditions, language, art, music, cuisine, and environment of a place, we open ourselves up to new perspectives, challenge our assumptions, and broaden our understanding of the world. As we embark on our travels, let us embrace the spirit of curiosity and learning, seeking knowledge that will illuminate our paths and enrich our lives.

ppp

Every destination has a story to tell, a culture to unveil, and an environment to protect. Educate yourself, embrace diversity, and let your curiosity guide you towards a deeper understanding of the world.

THIRTEEN

Volunteering and Giving Back: Contributing to Local Communities

Travel has the transformative power to broaden our horizons, challenge our assumptions, and connect us with diverse cultures and communities. Yet, as we embark on our journeys of discovery, it is essential to consider the impact we have on the places we visit. Responsible travelers recognize that travel is not merely about taking; it's also about giving back. Volunteering and contributing to local communities are integral aspects of sustainable tourism, enriching our travel experiences while leaving a positive legacy in the places we explore.

Volunteering and giving back are acts of reciprocity, acknowledging the hospitality and generosity of local communities while contributing to their well-being and development. It involves engaging in activities that benefit the local environment, economy, or social fabric. This can take many forms, such as working on conservation projects, teaching English in schools, supporting community-based tourism initiatives, or simply lending a helping hand wherever needed. By volunteering our time and skills, we not only contribute to meaningful projects but also forge deeper connections with local people and cultures.

The benefits of volunteering and giving back are manifold and extend far beyond the immediate impact on the community. For the volunteer, it offers a unique opportunity to learn new skills, gain a deeper understanding of different cultures and perspectives, and make a tangible difference in the lives of others. It can also be a personally rewarding experience, fostering a sense of purpose and fulfillment. For the community, volunteering can provide much-needed resources, expertise, and support, helping to address local challenges and promote sustainable development. It can also foster cultural exchange and understanding, building bridges between different communities and creating a more interconnected world.

There are numerous ways to volunteer and give back while traveling. One option is to participate in organized volunteer programs offered by various organizations and tour operators. These programs typically focus on specific areas, such as environmental conservation, community development, education, or healthcare. They provide volunteers with structured opportunities to contribute their skills and expertise to projects that align with their interests and values. Alternatively, travelers can choose to volunteer independently, seeking out local organizations or community initiatives that need support. This can involve working on farms, teaching English in schools, or assisting with community development projects.

Choosing responsible volunteer organizations is crucial to ensure that your efforts have a positive impact. Look for organizations that are transparent about their operations, have a clear mission and goals, and work in partnership with local communities. Avoid organizations that charge exorbitant fees, exploit volunteers, or engage in activities that may harm the environment or local culture. Do your research, read reviews from previous volunteers, and ask questions to ensure that your time and resources are being used effectively and ethically.

When volunteering abroad, it's essential to be culturally sensitive and respectful of local customs and traditions. This includes learning about the local culture, language, and social norms, dressing appropriately, and avoiding behaviors that may be considered offensive or disrespectful. It's also important to be mindful of your role as a volunteer, recognizing that you are there to support the community, not to impose your own values or beliefs. By approaching volunteering with humility and respect, you can create a more meaningful and mutually beneficial experience for both yourself and the community.

Volunteering and giving back are not limited to international travel; there are also many opportunities to contribute to your local community. This can involve volunteering at local shelters, food banks, or community centers, participating in environmental cleanups, or supporting local businesses and organizations. By giving back to your own community, you can strengthen social bonds, foster a sense of belonging, and create a more vibrant and resilient community.

In the context of sustainable travel, volunteering and giving back are not just optional activities; they are integral to responsible tourism. By contributing our time, skills, and resources to local communities, we can create a positive impact that extends far beyond our individual experiences. We can help to protect the environment, support sustainable development, and foster cross-cultural understanding. By embracing the spirit of giving, we can transform our travels into a force for good, leaving a legacy of positive change in the places we visit and the people we meet.

Volunteering and giving back are not just about doing good; they are also about personal growth and transformation. By stepping outside of our comfort zones and immersing ourselves in different cultures and communities, we can learn new skills, gain new perspectives, and broaden our understanding of the world. We can challenge our assumptions, expand our horizons, and develop a deeper sense of empathy and compassion. Volunteering and giving back are not just about what we give; they are also about what we receive.

ppp

Volunteering is a gift of time and talent, a bridge between cultures, and a catalyst for positive change. Give back to local communities, share your skills, and forge meaningful connections that enrich both lives.

FOURTEEN

LEAVING NO TRACE: PROTECTING NATURAL ENVIRONMENTS

As we venture into the embrace of nature, seeking solace, adventure, and connection, it is imperative to recognize our role as stewards of the environment. The principle of Leave No Trace (LNT) serves as a guiding light for responsible outdoor ethics, reminding us to minimize our impact and preserve the pristine beauty of natural environments. Leaving no trace is not merely a set of rules; it is a philosophy, a commitment to protecting the delicate balance of ecosystems and ensuring that future generations can experience the same untamed wonders that we have been fortunate enough to encounter.

At its core, Leave No Trace is a set of seven principles that provide a framework for minimizing our impact on the environment while enjoying outdoor activities. These principles encompass various aspects of responsible recreation, including planning and preparation, traveling and camping on durable surfaces, disposing of waste properly, minimizing campfire impacts, respecting wildlife, being considerate of other visitors, and leaving what we find. By adhering to these principles, we can ensure that our presence in nature leaves a minimal trace, allowing natural processes to unfold undisturbed.

The philosophy behind Leave No Trace is rooted in the understanding that our actions, no matter how small, can have a cumulative impact on the environment. Even seemingly insignificant actions, such as leaving behind a candy wrapper or straying off designated trails, can disrupt ecosystems, harm wildlife, and degrade the overall quality of natural areas. By adopting a Leave No Trace ethic, we acknowledge our responsibility to protect these fragile environments and act as stewards of the land.

The benefits of leaving no trace are manifold and extend far beyond the preservation of natural beauty. By minimizing our impact, we protect biodiversity, conserve water and energy, reduce pollution, and create a more sustainable future for all. Leaving no trace also enhances our own outdoor experiences by fostering a deeper connection with nature, promoting a sense of stewardship, and ensuring that future generations can enjoy the same pristine wilderness that we have been privileged to explore.

Planning and preparation are essential components of leaving no trace. Before embarking on any outdoor adventure, it is crucial to research the area, understand the local regulations and guidelines, and pack accordingly. This includes packing out all trash and waste, carrying reusable containers and utensils, and choosing eco-friendly products that minimize environmental impact. By planning and preparing thoughtfully, we can minimize our footprint and ensure that our presence in nature is a positive one.

Traveling and camping on durable surfaces is another key principle of Leave No Trace. This means sticking to established trails and campsites, avoiding trampling vegetation, and minimizing the impact on fragile ecosystems. When camping, choose designated campsites or areas that can withstand the impact of human activity. Avoid camping near water sources, as this can contaminate water and disturb wildlife. By traveling and camping responsibly, we can protect the integrity of natural areas and preserve their beauty for future generations.

Proper disposal of waste is essential for leaving no trace. This includes packing out all trash, food scraps, and litter, even biodegradable items such as apple cores or banana peels. These items can take a long time to decompose and can attract wildlife, leading to undesirable interactions. It also means using established restrooms or catholes for human waste, following proper hygiene practices, and disposing of wastewater responsibly. By properly disposing of waste, we can prevent pollution, protect water sources, and maintain the cleanliness of natural areas.

Minimizing campfire impacts is another important aspect of leaving no trace. Campfires can be a source of enjoyment and warmth, but they can also cause significant damage to the environment if not managed properly. If campfires are permitted, use established fire rings or fire pans, keep fires small and manageable, and burn only wood that is dead and down. Never leave a fire unattended, and ensure that it is completely extinguished before leaving the area. Consider using a camp stove for cooking, as this can be a more environmentally friendly option.

Respecting wildlife is crucial for maintaining the ecological balance of natural environments. Observe animals from a distance, avoid approaching or feeding them, and keep pets under control. Remember, we are visitors in their homes, and it is our responsibility to minimize our impact on their natural behaviors and habitats. By respecting wildlife, we can ensure their well-being and contribute to the preservation of biodiversity.

Being considerate of other visitors is an essential aspect of responsible recreation. Keep noise levels down, avoid disturbing other campers or hikers, and yield to others on trails. Respect the solitude and tranquility that many people seek in nature. By being considerate of others, we can create a more enjoyable and harmonious outdoor experience for everyone.

Leaving what we find is a fundamental principle of Leave No Trace. This means leaving rocks, plants, and other natural objects as we find them, resisting the urge to collect souvenirs or disturb the natural landscape. It also means avoiding introducing or transporting invasive species, which can have devastating consequences for ecosystems. By leaving what we find, we preserve the natural beauty and integrity of the environment for others to enjoy.

In conclusion, leaving no trace is more than just a set of rules; it is a philosophy, a commitment to protecting and preserving the natural world. By adhering to the seven principles of Leave No Trace, we can minimize our impact on the environment, protect biodiversity, and ensure that future generations can experience the same untamed wonders that we have been fortunate enough to encounter. Leaving no trace is not just about what we do; it's about who we are as responsible travelers and stewards of the earth.

Tread lightly on the earth, leaving only footprints and taking only memories. Embrace Leave No Trace principles, minimize your impact, and preserve the pristine beauty of natural environments for generations to come.

FIFTEEN

TRAVELING BY FOOT OR BIKE: EXPLORING AT A SLOWER PACE

In a world that often prioritizes speed and efficiency, the allure of slow travel beckons those seeking a more immersive and mindful way to explore the world. Traveling by foot or bike allows us to break free from the confines of conventional transportation, offering a unique opportunity to engage with our surroundings at a slower pace. This unhurried approach to travel not only reduces our environmental impact but also opens doors to unexpected encounters, deeper connections, and a renewed appreciation for the journey itself.

Traveling by foot or bike is a celebration of simplicity, a return to the roots of exploration. It allows us to reconnect with our bodies, to feel the rhythm of our footsteps on the earth or the wind in our hair as we pedal along. It invites us to slow down, to savor the details, and to appreciate the subtle nuances of our surroundings. It is a journey of the senses, where every sight, sound, and smell becomes more vivid and profound. By embracing a slower pace, we open ourselves up to the transformative power of travel, allowing it to touch our hearts and minds in profound ways.

The benefits of traveling by foot or bike are numerous and extend far beyond the physical act of movement. It is a sustainable mode of transportation, reducing our carbon footprint and minimizing our impact on the environment. It also promotes physical and mental well-being, offering a low-impact form of exercise that strengthens our bodies and calms our minds. Additionally, it fosters a deeper connection with the places we visit, as we interact with locals, observe daily life, and discover hidden gems that might be missed when traveling at a faster pace.

Traveling by foot offers a unique perspective on the world. It allows us to explore at our own pace, to linger in places that capture our imagination, and to forge serendipitous encounters with locals and fellow travelers. Whether it's a leisurely stroll through a historic city center, a challenging hike in the mountains, or a pilgrimage along an ancient trail, walking opens up a world of possibilities for exploration and discovery. It allows us to experience the world through our senses, to feel the texture of the earth beneath our feet, to smell the aromas of local cuisine wafting through the air, and to hear the sounds of nature and culture mingling in harmony.

Cycling, on the other hand, offers a unique blend of freedom and adventure. It allows us to cover greater distances than walking, opening up vast landscapes and diverse terrains for exploration. Whether it's a leisurely ride through a picturesque countryside, a challenging climb up a mountain pass, or a multi-day cycling tour along a scenic route, cycling offers a thrilling and rewarding way to experience the world. It allows us to feel the wind in our hair, the sun on our skin, and the exhilaration of propelling ourselves forward through sheer human power.

Both walking and cycling offer unique opportunities for cultural immersion. By traveling at a slower pace, we have the chance to interact with locals, to learn about their customs and traditions, and to experience their daily lives firsthand. We can stop at roadside stalls to sample local delicacies, chat with farmers in their fields, or join a local festival or celebration. By immersing ourselves in the local culture, we gain a deeper understanding of the places we visit and forge connections that transcend the boundaries of language and nationality.

In addition to its cultural and environmental benefits, traveling by foot or bike also offers a sense of freedom and autonomy that is often lacking in conventional modes of transportation. We are not bound by schedules, routes, or timetables. We can go where we want, when we want, and at our own pace. This freedom allows us to truly embrace the spirit of adventure, to explore the world on our own terms, and to create our own unique and unforgettable travel experiences.

Of course, traveling by foot or bike requires some preparation and planning. It is important to choose appropriate gear and clothing, pack light, and be prepared for varying weather conditions. It is also essential to research the route, understand the terrain and elevation changes, and ensure that you have the necessary skills and experience for the chosen activity. However, with proper preparation, traveling by foot or bike can be a safe and enjoyable way to explore the world.

In conclusion, traveling by foot or bike offers a refreshing alternative to the fast-paced, consumer-driven model of tourism that dominates much of the modern world. It is a slower, more mindful way to travel, allowing us to connect with our surroundings, engage with local communities, and experience the world through our senses. It is a sustainable and responsible mode of transportation that reduces our environmental impact and promotes physical and mental well-being. Whether you choose to hike through a national park, cycle along a scenic coastline, or simply stroll through a historic city center, traveling by foot or bike offers a unique and rewarding way to explore the world and discover its hidden treasures.

ᐳᐳᐳ

Traveling by foot or bike awakens your senses and deepens your connection with the world. Slow down, breathe in the fresh air, and let each step or pedal stroke reveal the hidden treasures of your journey.

SIXTEEN
AVOIDING SINGLE-USE PLASTICS: CHOOSING REUSABLE ALTERNATIVES

In our modern world, convenience often comes wrapped in plastic. Single-use plastics, designed for fleeting moments of use before being discarded, have permeated nearly every aspect of our lives. From disposable cutlery and water bottles to plastic bags and packaging, these ubiquitous items have become a symbol of our throwaway culture. However, as awareness of the devastating impact of plastic pollution grows, a movement towards sustainable alternatives is gaining momentum. As mindful travelers, we have the power to make a difference by avoiding single-use plastics and choosing reusable alternatives, both at home and on our journeys.

Avoiding single-use plastics is not merely a trend; it's a conscious choice that reflects our commitment to environmental stewardship and sustainable living. Single-use plastics pose a significant threat to our planet, polluting our oceans, harming wildlife, and contributing to climate change. By reducing our reliance on these disposable items, we can lessen our ecological footprint and create a healthier planet for future generations. It's a small but powerful step towards a more sustainable future, one that starts with our individual choices and actions.

The environmental impact of single-use plastics is staggering. Billions of plastic items are produced and discarded each year, ending up in landfills, incinerators, or the environment. Plastic takes hundreds of years to decompose, releasing harmful chemicals into the soil and water as it breaks down. It also pollutes our oceans, harming marine life and entering the food chain. Additionally, the production of plastic contributes to greenhouse gas emissions, exacerbating climate change. By avoiding single-use plastics, we can help mitigate these environmental consequences and create a more sustainable future.

Choosing reusable alternatives is a simple yet impactful way to reduce our plastic footprint. Instead of reaching for a disposable water bottle, carry a reusable one made of stainless steel, glass, or BPA-free plastic. Instead of using plastic bags, bring a reusable tote bag for shopping or packing. Invest in reusable food containers, cutlery, straws, and coffee cups. These simple swaps can significantly reduce the amount of plastic waste we generate. By making these conscious choices, we not only minimize our environmental impact but also set an example for others to follow.

Packing reusable alternatives is particularly important while traveling. When we are on the go, it can be tempting to opt for convenience and reach for disposable items. However, by packing a few essential reusable items, we can avoid contributing to plastic pollution while exploring new destinations. A reusable water bottle, for instance, can be filled up at water fountains or refilling stations, eliminating the need for single-use plastic bottles. A reusable coffee cup can be used at cafes and restaurants, reducing the demand for disposable cups. By packing reusable alternatives, we can ensure that our travels are more sustainable and responsible.

Supporting businesses and initiatives that prioritize sustainability is another important aspect of avoiding single-use plastics. Many businesses are now offering reusable options, such as refillable containers for food and beverages, or discounts for customers who bring their own bags or cups. By choosing to patronize these businesses, we can encourage more sustainable practices and send a message to other businesses that consumers are demanding more environmentally friendly options.

Beyond individual actions, advocating for policy changes that reduce plastic production and promote recycling and reuse is crucial. Supporting organizations and campaigns that work to tackle plastic pollution can amplify our impact and contribute to systemic change. By raising awareness about the issue, supporting legislation that restricts single-use plastics, and promoting sustainable alternatives, we can create a world where plastic pollution is no longer a threat to our planet.

Avoiding single-use plastics is not just about changing our habits; it's about changing our mindset. It's about shifting away from a throwaway culture and embracing a more mindful and sustainable approach to consumption. It's about recognizing the interconnectedness of our actions and their impact on the environment. By choosing reusable alternatives, supporting sustainable businesses, and advocating for policy changes, we can create a future where plastic pollution is a thing of the past.

In conclusion, avoiding single-use plastics and choosing reusable alternatives is a powerful way to reduce our environmental impact and contribute to a more sustainable future. By making conscious choices about the products we use, the businesses we support, and the policies we advocate for, we can create a world where plastic pollution is no longer a threat to our planet. It's a journey of awareness, education, and action, a journey that can transform our lives and the world around us. By embracing reusable alternatives, we not only protect the environment but also inspire others to do the same, creating a ripple effect of positive change.

Refuse single-use plastics and embrace the power of reusable alternatives. Choose sustainable options, from water bottles and coffee cups to shopping bags and food containers, and be part of the solution to plastic pollution.

SEVENTEEN

Shopping Responsibly: Avoiding Souvenirs with Negative Impacts

Travel has long been associated with the thrill of discovering new cultures and bringing home tangible memories of our adventures. Souvenirs serve as tokens of our experiences, connecting us to the places we've visited and the people we've met. However, the act of shopping for souvenirs can have unintended consequences, both for the environment and local communities. As mindful travelers, we have a responsibility to shop responsibly, choosing souvenirs that do not harm the environment, exploit local artisans, or perpetuate unsustainable practices.

Responsible shopping is a conscious choice that considers the ethical, social, and environmental impact of our purchases. It involves researching the origins of products, understanding the production processes involved, and supporting businesses that prioritize sustainability and fair trade. By shopping responsibly, we can ensure that our souvenirs are not only meaningful keepsakes but also contribute to the well-being of the planet and its inhabitants. It's about making choices that align with our values and leave a positive impact on the places we visit.

The impact of irresponsible souvenir shopping can be far-reaching and detrimental. The demand for certain souvenirs, such as those made from endangered species or rare materials, can fuel illegal wildlife trade, habitat destruction, and environmental degradation. Additionally, mass-produced souvenirs often contribute to overconsumption, waste generation, and carbon emissions associated with transportation. Furthermore, purchasing souvenirs from exploitative businesses can perpetuate unfair labor practices and undermine local economies. By being mindful of our choices, we can avoid contributing to these negative impacts and support a more sustainable and ethical tourism model.

One of the fundamental principles of responsible shopping is to avoid souvenirs made from endangered species or materials that harm the environment. This includes items made from ivory, coral, tortoise shell, or other animal products sourced from illegal wildlife trade. It also includes souvenirs made from unsustainable materials, such as rare woods, minerals, or gemstones extracted through environmentally destructive practices. By avoiding these items, we can help protect endangered species and preserve their habitats, ensuring their survival for future generations.

Researching the origins of souvenirs is crucial for responsible shopping. Before purchasing an item, inquire about its source, the materials used, and the production process involved. Ask questions about the working conditions of the artisans or producers, the environmental impact of the production process, and the cultural significance of the item. Many reputable shops and artisans are transparent about their practices and are happy to share information about their products. By doing our research, we can make informed decisions about our purchases and ensure that our souvenirs are ethically sourced and produced.

Supporting local artisans and businesses is another key aspect of responsible shopping. By purchasing souvenirs directly from local artisans, we contribute to the local economy, empower local communities, and preserve traditional crafts and skills. Look for locally made handicrafts, artwork, textiles, or other products that reflect the unique culture and heritage of the destination. These items not only serve as meaningful souvenirs but also support the livelihoods of local artisans and their families.

Choosing souvenirs that are made from sustainable materials is another important consideration. Look for items made from recycled materials, natural fibers, or other eco-friendly alternatives. Avoid souvenirs made from plastic, as plastic pollution is a major environmental problem. Additionally, consider the durability and longevity of the souvenir. Choosing high-quality items that will last for years to come can reduce waste and minimize the need for frequent replacements.

Beyond avoiding harmful souvenirs, responsible shopping also involves being mindful of our consumption habits. Overconsumption of souvenirs can contribute to waste generation and environmental degradation. Instead of buying numerous trinkets and souvenirs, focus on choosing a few meaningful items that you will cherish and use. Consider experiences as souvenirs, such as taking a cooking class, learning a traditional craft, or participating in a cultural activity. These experiences not only create lasting memories but also support local businesses and communities.

When shopping for souvenirs, it's important to be aware of cultural sensitivities and avoid purchasing items that may be considered offensive or inappropriate. This includes items that depict religious figures, sacred symbols, or culturally sensitive images. It's also important to respect intellectual property rights and avoid purchasing counterfeit or imitation products, as these can undermine the livelihoods of local artisans and businesses.

In conclusion, responsible souvenir shopping is an integral part of sustainable travel. By avoiding souvenirs with negative impacts, researching the origins of products, supporting local artisans and businesses, choosing sustainable materials, and being mindful of our consumption habits, we can ensure that our purchases contribute to the well-being of the planet and its inhabitants. Responsible shopping is not just about what we buy; it's about how we buy and the impact of our choices. By making conscious decisions about our purchases, we can transform our souvenir shopping into a positive force for good, supporting sustainable practices, preserving cultural heritage, and empowering local communities.

ᐁᐁᐁ

Shopping responsibly is an act of conscious consumerism. Research the origins of souvenirs, support local artisans, and choose sustainable materials that reflect your values and minimize your impact.

EIGHTEEN

SUPPORTING CONSERVATION EFFORTS: VISITING NATIONAL PARKS AND RESERVES

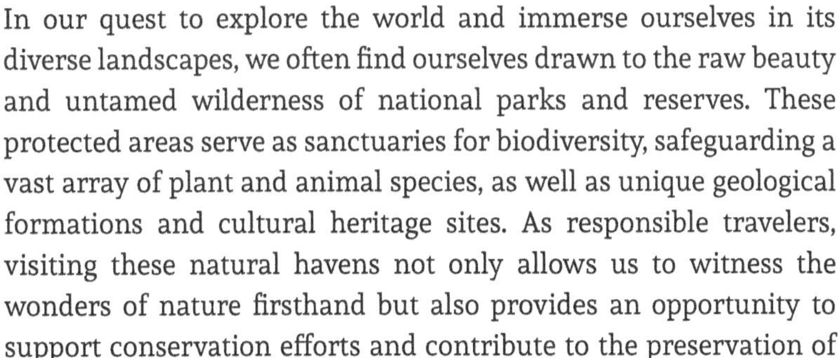

In our quest to explore the world and immerse ourselves in its diverse landscapes, we often find ourselves drawn to the raw beauty and untamed wilderness of national parks and reserves. These protected areas serve as sanctuaries for biodiversity, safeguarding a vast array of plant and animal species, as well as unique geological formations and cultural heritage sites. As responsible travelers, visiting these natural havens not only allows us to witness the wonders of nature firsthand but also provides an opportunity to support conservation efforts and contribute to the preservation of our planet's ecological treasures.

National parks and reserves play a pivotal role in protecting biodiversity and maintaining ecological balance. They provide a safe haven for countless species, including endangered and threatened ones, shielding them from habitat loss, poaching, and other human-induced threats. These protected areas also serve as living laboratories for scientific research, allowing scientists to study ecosystems, monitor wildlife populations, and develop strategies for conservation and management. By visiting these parks and reserves, we not only gain a deeper understanding of the natural world but also contribute to the funding and support needed for their continued protection.

The benefits of supporting conservation efforts through visiting national parks and reserves are far-reaching and multifaceted. It helps protect endangered species and their habitats, ensuring their survival for future generations. It preserves biodiversity, which is essential for maintaining ecological balance and providing vital ecosystem services, such as clean air and water, pollination, and climate regulation. It also supports local communities, as many parks and reserves provide employment opportunities and contribute to the local economy through tourism. By visiting these protected areas, we become part of a global movement to safeguard our planet's natural heritage.

Choosing national parks and reserves that prioritize conservation is a crucial step in supporting these efforts. Look for parks and reserves that have robust management plans, engage in scientific research and monitoring, and actively participate in community outreach and education programs. Many parks and reserves have visitor centers or information booths where you can learn about their conservation initiatives and how you can contribute. Additionally, consider supporting parks and reserves that are part of larger conservation networks or initiatives, such as UNESCO World Heritage Sites or Biosphere Reserves, as these designations often signify a high level of commitment to conservation and sustainable development.

Paying park entrance fees and supporting local businesses is a direct way to contribute to conservation efforts. Entrance fees often go towards funding park operations, maintenance, and conservation programs. By paying these fees, we directly support the management and protection of the park and its resources. Additionally, patronizing local businesses, such as restaurants, shops, and tour operators that adhere to sustainable practices, can further contribute to the local economy and support conservation efforts.

Volunteering for conservation projects is another meaningful way to contribute to the preservation of national parks and reserves. Many parks and reserves offer volunteer programs that allow visitors to participate in various conservation activities, such as trail maintenance, wildlife monitoring, habitat restoration, and environmental education. By volunteering our time and skills, we not only help to protect the environment but also gain a deeper understanding of the challenges and rewards of conservation work.

Responsible behavior while visiting national parks and reserves is crucial for minimizing our impact and preserving the natural environment. This includes following park rules and regulations, staying on designated trails, avoiding disturbing wildlife, and packing out all trash and waste. It also means being mindful of our noise levels, minimizing light pollution, and respecting the cultural heritage of indigenous communities who may have a deep connection to the land. By practicing responsible tourism, we can ensure that our visits to national parks and reserves are not only enjoyable but also sustainable.

Spreading awareness about conservation efforts is another important way to support national parks and reserves. Share your experiences on social media, write reviews on travel platforms, and encourage others to visit and support these protected areas. By raising awareness about the importance of conservation and the threats facing these natural havens, we can inspire others to take action and contribute to their protection.

Supporting conservation organizations is another effective way to contribute to the preservation of national parks and reserves. Many non-profit organizations work tirelessly to protect endangered species, restore habitats, and promote sustainable tourism. By donating to these organizations, we can provide much-needed funding for their conservation efforts and help them continue their vital work.

In conclusion, supporting conservation efforts through visiting national parks and reserves is a powerful way to contribute to the preservation of our planet's natural heritage. By choosing parks and reserves that prioritize conservation, paying park entrance fees, supporting local businesses, volunteering for conservation projects, practicing responsible behavior, spreading awareness, and supporting conservation organizations, we can make a real difference in protecting biodiversity, preserving ecosystems, and ensuring that future generations can experience the wonders of nature. It is a collective responsibility that requires our commitment and action, a responsibility that we can fulfill through our travels and our everyday choices.

ppp

National parks and reserves are sanctuaries of biodiversity, deserving of our protection and support. Pay entrance fees, volunteer your time, and choose responsible tour operators to ensure their preservation.

NINETEEN
Choosing Sustainable Tour Operators: Researching Before Booking

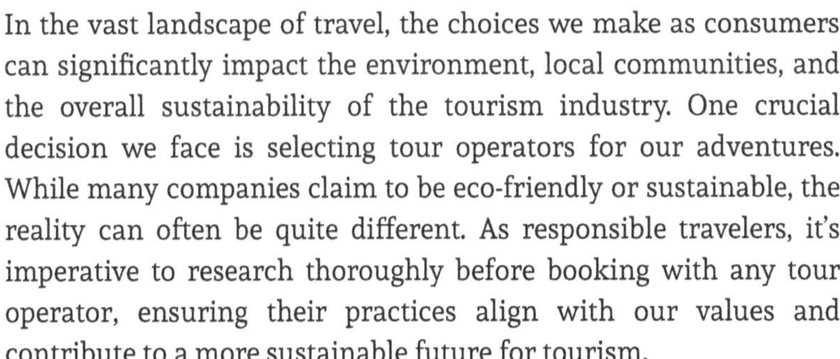

In the vast landscape of travel, the choices we make as consumers can significantly impact the environment, local communities, and the overall sustainability of the tourism industry. One crucial decision we face is selecting tour operators for our adventures. While many companies claim to be eco-friendly or sustainable, the reality can often be quite different. As responsible travelers, it's imperative to research thoroughly before booking with any tour operator, ensuring their practices align with our values and contribute to a more sustainable future for tourism.

Choosing sustainable tour operators is not merely a matter of personal preference; it's a conscious decision that can have a ripple effect on the entire industry. By supporting companies that prioritize environmental protection, social responsibility, and economic empowerment, we send a powerful message to the market. We demonstrate that travelers are demanding more sustainable options and are willing to invest in companies that prioritize ethical practices. This, in turn, can incentivize other tour operators to adopt more sustainable practices, creating a positive feedback loop that benefits both the environment and local communities.

The benefits of choosing sustainable tour operators are manifold and extend far beyond the individual traveler. Sustainable tourism can contribute to the preservation of natural habitats and wildlife, support local economies, empower communities, and promote cultural exchange and understanding. By opting for tours that minimize environmental impact, respect local cultures, and provide fair wages and working conditions for employees, we can ensure that our travels leave a positive legacy in the destinations we visit. Additionally, sustainable tour operators often offer unique and authentic experiences that allow us to connect more deeply with the places we explore, fostering a greater appreciation for their natural and cultural heritage.

Researching before booking is the key to identifying truly sustainable tour operators. Start by looking for certifications and accreditations from reputable organizations, such as the Global Sustainable Tourism Council (GSTC). These certifications indicate that the company has met rigorous standards for sustainability, including environmental protection, social responsibility, and economic viability. Additionally, look for tour operators that are members of organizations that promote sustainable tourism, such as the International Ecotourism Society (TIES) or the Adventure Travel Trade Association (ATTA). These organizations often have codes of conduct and sustainability guidelines that their members must adhere to.

Delving deeper into a tour operator's website and marketing materials can reveal further insights into their sustainability practices. Look for detailed information about their environmental policies, such as their efforts to minimize waste, conserve water and energy, and reduce carbon emissions. They should also provide information about their social responsibility initiatives, such as their support for local communities, fair trade practices, and efforts to preserve cultural heritage. Transparent communication about their sustainability efforts is a positive sign that the company is committed to responsible tourism.

Reading reviews and testimonials from previous customers can provide valuable insights into a tour operator's practices and reputation. Look for reviews that mention specific sustainability initiatives, such as eco-friendly accommodations, locally sourced food, and support for community projects. Pay attention to both positive and negative reviews, as they can offer a balanced perspective on the company's strengths and weaknesses. Additionally, consider seeking recommendations from friends, family, or online forums dedicated to sustainable travel. These personal recommendations can be invaluable in identifying tour operators that align with your values and priorities.

When evaluating a tour operator's sustainability, consider their transportation choices, accommodation options, and activities offered. Sustainable tour operators prioritize low-impact transportation options, such as walking, cycling, public transportation, or fuel-efficient vehicles. They also choose accommodations that have implemented sustainable practices, such as energy and water conservation measures, waste reduction programs, and support for local communities. The activities offered should also be environmentally and culturally responsible, avoiding activities that harm wildlife or exploit local cultures.

It's important to note that sustainability is an ongoing process, and even the most well-intentioned tour operators may have room for improvement. Don't hesitate to ask questions and seek clarification about their practices. Inquire about their environmental policies, social responsibility initiatives, and future sustainability goals. A transparent and open dialogue with the tour operator can help you make an informed decision and ensure that your travels align with your values.

In conclusion, choosing sustainable tour operators is a crucial step in promoting responsible tourism and minimizing our environmental impact. By researching before booking, we can identify companies that prioritize sustainability, support local communities, and offer authentic and meaningful travel experiences. This involves looking for certifications and accreditations, delving into their marketing materials and websites, reading reviews and testimonials, and asking questions about their practices. By making informed choices and supporting sustainable tour operators, we can contribute to a more ethical and sustainable tourism industry that benefits both travelers and the destinations they visit.

ϼϼϼ

Choosing a sustainable tour operator is an investment in responsible tourism. Research certifications, read reviews, and ask questions to ensure your adventure aligns with your values and minimizes its environmental footprint.

TWENTY

SPREADING THE WORD: ENCOURAGING OTHERS TO TRAVEL SUSTAINABLY

Travel has an undeniable power to connect us with the world, fostering cultural exchange, personal growth, and unforgettable memories. However, as the popularity of travel continues to rise, so does its impact on the environment and local communities. As mindful travelers, we have a responsibility to not only minimize our own footprint but also inspire and encourage others to embrace sustainable travel practices. Spreading the word about sustainable tourism is not just an act of advocacy; it's an invitation to create a collective movement that transforms the way we explore the world.

Spreading the word about sustainable tourism is a multifaceted endeavor that involves education, communication, and advocacy. It's about raising awareness about the environmental and social impacts of travel, promoting responsible practices, and inspiring others to make conscious choices that benefit both the planet and its inhabitants. It's about sharing our experiences, knowledge, and passion for sustainable travel, and encouraging others to join us on this journey towards a more responsible and ethical form of tourism.

The power of spreading the word lies in its ability to create a ripple effect of positive change. By sharing our stories, insights, and experiences, we can inspire others to rethink their travel habits and adopt more sustainable practices. We can spark conversations, challenge assumptions, and create a community of like-minded individuals who are committed to protecting the environment and supporting local communities through their travels. By amplifying our voices and collaborating with others, we can create a movement that transforms the tourism industry and ensures a sustainable future for travel.

One of the most effective ways to spread the word about sustainable tourism is through storytelling. Sharing our personal experiences and the lessons we've learned along the way can be incredibly powerful in inspiring others. Whether it's through blog posts, social media posts, or conversations with friends and family, sharing our stories can humanize the concept of sustainable travel and make it more relatable and accessible to others. By highlighting the positive impacts of responsible travel, we can encourage others to embrace these practices and make a difference in their own travels.

Educating others about the environmental and social impacts of travel is another crucial aspect of spreading the word. This involves raising awareness about issues such as carbon emissions, waste generation, overtourism, and the exploitation of local communities. By providing accurate and accessible information about these challenges, we can empower individuals to make informed decisions about their travel choices and advocate for more sustainable practices. This can involve sharing articles, documentaries, and other resources that shed light on the environmental and social costs of travel, as well as highlighting the positive impacts of sustainable tourism.

Promoting responsible travel practices is essential in encouraging others to adopt a more sustainable approach to travel. This can involve sharing tips and advice on how to minimize one's environmental footprint, such as choosing eco-friendly accommodations, reducing waste, conserving water and energy, and supporting local businesses and communities. It can also involve advocating for more sustainable transportation options, such as public transportation, cycling, or walking, and encouraging travelers to consider the impact of their choices on the environment and local communities.

Collaboration and community building are key to amplifying the message of sustainable tourism. By partnering with like-minded individuals, organizations, and businesses, we can create a network of support and resources for those who are interested in traveling more sustainably. This can involve organizing workshops and events, participating in online forums and discussions, and collaborating on projects that promote sustainable tourism practices. By working together, we can create a collective voice that advocates for change and inspires a wider audience to embrace responsible travel.

In the digital age, social media platforms offer a powerful tool for spreading the word about sustainable tourism. By sharing photos, videos, and stories about our sustainable travel experiences, we can reach a wide audience and inspire others to follow suit. Social media can also be used to connect with like-minded individuals, share resources and information, and create a community of sustainable travelers who support and encourage each other. However, it's important to use social media responsibly, ensuring that our messages are accurate, informative, and respectful of different perspectives.

Spreading the word about sustainable tourism is not just about preaching to the choir; it's about engaging with a diverse audience and finding common ground. It's about starting conversations, listening to different viewpoints, and finding solutions that work for everyone. It's about creating a movement that is inclusive, welcoming, and accessible to all, regardless of their background, experience, or budget. By fostering a sense of community and shared purpose, we can create a powerful force for positive change in the tourism industry.

In conclusion, spreading the word about sustainable tourism is a responsibility that we all share as travelers and global citizens. By educating ourselves and others about the environmental and social impacts of travel, promoting responsible practices, and collaborating with like-minded individuals and organizations, we can create a movement that transforms the way we explore the world. It's a journey of awareness, education, and action, a journey that can lead to a more sustainable, equitable, and fulfilling travel experience for all.

ᐅᐅᐅ

Be an ambassador for sustainable travel. Share your experiences, inspire others, and advocate for practices that protect the planet and empower local communities.

TWENTY-ONE

REFLECTING ON YOUR IMPACT: EVALUATING AND IMPROVING YOUR PRACTICES

In the ever-evolving journey of sustainable travel, reflection serves as a compass, guiding us towards a deeper understanding of our impact and inspiring us to continuously improve our practices. It is a process of introspection, evaluation, and learning, where we examine our choices, actions, and their consequences. By reflecting on our impact, we not only gain valuable insights into our own behavior but also contribute to the collective effort to create a more responsible and sustainable tourism industry.

Reflecting on our impact as travelers is not merely an exercise in self-criticism; it's a process of growth and learning. It's about acknowledging that we are not perfect, that we may have made choices that could have been more sustainable or responsible.

However, instead of dwelling on past mistakes, reflection allows us to learn from them, to identify areas for improvement, and to make more conscious choices in the future. It's a continuous journey of self-awareness and growth, one that can lead to a more meaningful and fulfilling travel experience.

The benefits of reflecting on our impact are numerous and profound. It can help us become more aware of the environmental and social consequences of our travel choices, leading to more responsible behavior. It can inspire us to seek out more sustainable options, such as eco-friendly accommodations, local food, and low-impact transportation. It can also foster a deeper connection with the places we visit and the people we meet, as we become more mindful of our interactions and impact. By reflecting on our impact, we not only transform our own travels but also contribute to a more sustainable and equitable tourism industry.

The process of reflection can begin with asking ourselves some fundamental questions. What impact did our travels have on the environment? Did we contribute to the local economy? Did we engage with local communities in a respectful and meaningful way? Did we learn anything new about ourselves or the world around us? These questions can serve as a starting point for a deeper exploration of our travel experiences and their impact.

Evaluating our environmental impact involves examining our carbon footprint, waste generation, and resource consumption. Did we choose transportation options that minimized our carbon emissions? Did we reduce our waste by using reusable containers, water bottles, and bags? Did we conserve water and energy in our accommodations and activities? By assessing our environmental impact, we can identify areas where we can make improvements and adopt more sustainable practices in the future.

Assessing our social impact involves considering our interactions with local communities. Did we support local businesses and artisans? Did we engage in cultural exchange and learn about local traditions and customs? Did we respect local norms and values? By reflecting on our social impact, we can gain a deeper understanding of our role as travelers and the impact we have on the places we visit.

Reflection is not just about identifying areas for improvement; it's also about celebrating our successes and acknowledging the positive impact we have made. Perhaps we chose eco-friendly accommodations, volunteered for a local project, or simply took the time to connect with locals and learn about their culture. These positive experiences can serve as motivation to continue our journey towards more sustainable and responsible travel.

Documenting our reflections can be a helpful way to track our progress and identify patterns in our behavior. This can be done through journaling, blogging, or simply keeping notes on our travels. By recording our thoughts, feelings, and observations, we create a valuable resource for future reference and can gain deeper insights into our own growth and development as travelers.

Sharing our reflections with others can also be a powerful way to inspire and educate others. By sharing our stories, insights, and experiences, we can encourage others to adopt more sustainable and responsible travel practices. We can spark conversations, challenge assumptions, and create a community of like-minded individuals who are committed to creating a more positive impact through their travels.

In conclusion, reflecting on our impact as travelers is a crucial step in the journey towards sustainable tourism. It is a process of self-awareness, evaluation, and learning, where we examine our choices, actions, and their consequences. By reflecting on our impact, we can identify areas for improvement, adopt more sustainable practices, and create a more positive legacy in the places we visit. It is a continuous journey of growth and transformation, one that can lead to a more meaningful, fulfilling, and responsible travel experience.

ᐁᐁᐁ

Reflection is a compass guiding us towards a more sustainable path. Evaluate your choices, learn from your experiences, and strive to improve your practices with each journey.

TWENTY-TWO

CREATING A SUSTAINABLE TRAVEL PLAN: PLANNING MINDFULLY FOR FUTURE ADVENTURES

the tapestry of travel, planning is the brushstroke that shapes our adventures, transforming dreams into reality. However, as conscientious travelers, we understand that our journeys have an impact on the environment and the communities we encounter. Creating a sustainable travel plan is not merely about logistics and itineraries; it's a conscious decision to prioritize responsible choices that minimize our footprint and contribute to a more sustainable future for tourism. By planning mindfully, we can embark on future adventures that enrich our lives while preserving the planet's natural and cultural treasures.

Sustainable travel planning begins with a shift in mindset, a recognition that our choices as travelers have consequences. It involves a commitment to minimizing our negative impact and maximizing our positive contributions. This shift in perspective requires us to rethink our priorities, to prioritize experiences over consumption, connection over convenience, and sustainability over short-term gains. By embracing this mindful approach to planning, we can create travel experiences that are not only enjoyable and fulfilling but also responsible and ethical.

The benefits of creating a sustainable travel plan are manifold and extend far beyond personal satisfaction. It allows us to reduce our carbon footprint by choosing eco-friendly transportation and accommodations, minimize waste generation by packing reusable items and supporting businesses that prioritize sustainability, and contribute to local economies by choosing locally owned businesses and supporting community-based tourism initiatives. It also enables us to engage with local cultures more authentically, fostering cross-cultural understanding and creating a more positive impact on the places we visit.

The first step in creating a sustainable travel plan is to choose a destination that aligns with our values and priorities. Research destinations that have a strong commitment to sustainability, such as those that have implemented eco-friendly policies, protected natural areas, and supported local communities. Consider visiting destinations that are off the beaten path, as this can help alleviate the pressures of overtourism and support local economies in lesser-known areas. By choosing destinations that prioritize sustainability, we can ensure that our travels contribute to a positive impact.

Once you have chosen your destination, the next step is to plan your transportation. Opt for low-impact transportation options whenever possible, such as trains, buses, or ferries, which generally have a lower carbon footprint than airplanes. If flying is unavoidable, consider carbon offsetting programs to compensate for your emissions. Research local transportation options at your destination, such as public transportation or bicycle rentals, to minimize your reliance on taxis or private cars. By choosing sustainable transportation options, you can significantly reduce your carbon footprint and contribute to a cleaner environment.

Choosing eco-friendly accommodations is another crucial aspect of sustainable travel planning. Look for hotels, guesthouses, or homestays that have implemented sustainable practices, such as energy and water conservation measures, waste reduction programs, and support for local communities. Consider staying in accommodations that are certified by reputable organizations, such as LEED (Leadership in Energy and Environmental Design) or Green Globe, which indicate a high level of commitment to sustainability. By choosing eco-friendly accommodations, you can minimize your environmental impact and support businesses that are committed to responsible tourism.

Packing responsibly is essential for minimizing waste and reducing your environmental footprint. Pack light by choosing versatile clothing items that can be mixed and matched to create different outfits. Bring reusable water bottles, coffee cups, food containers, and shopping bags to avoid single-use plastics. Choose toiletries and personal care products that are eco-friendly and packaged in recyclable or reusable containers. By packing responsibly, you can minimize your waste generation and contribute to a cleaner environment.

Planning your activities and excursions in advance can also help you make more sustainable choices. Research local tour operators and activities that prioritize sustainability, such as those that focus on ecotourism, cultural exchange, or community development.

Look for tours that use low-impact transportation, support local businesses, and minimize their environmental footprint. Consider participating in activities that allow you to give back to the community, such as volunteering for a local project or supporting a conservation initiative. By choosing sustainable activities, you can ensure that your travels have a positive impact on the environment and local communities.

Eating local is another important aspect of sustainable travel. By choosing locally sourced food and beverages, you can reduce the carbon footprint associated with food transportation, support local farmers and producers, and experience the unique flavors of the region. Look for restaurants that prioritize seasonal and organic ingredients, and avoid establishments that serve endangered species or unsustainable seafood. By eating local, you can contribute to the local economy, reduce your environmental impact, and indulge in a culinary adventure.

Minimizing waste throughout your journey is crucial for sustainable travel. Carry a reusable water bottle and refill it at water fountains or filtered water stations. Use reusable coffee cups, food containers, and shopping bags. Avoid single-use plastics, such as straws, cutlery, and condiment packets. Dispose of waste properly by recycling and composting whenever possible. By minimizing waste, you can reduce your environmental impact and contribute to a cleaner planet.

In conclusion, creating a sustainable travel plan is a conscious choice that empowers us to minimize our environmental footprint, support local communities, and create a positive impact through our travels. By choosing sustainable destinations, transportation, accommodations, and activities, packing responsibly, eating local, and minimizing waste, we can transform our journeys into a force for good. Sustainable travel is not just about doing less harm; it's about doing more good. It's about creating a new paradigm for tourism, one that prioritizes environmental protection, social responsibility, and economic empowerment.

❧❧❧

A sustainable travel plan is a roadmap to a responsible adventure. Choose eco-conscious options, minimize waste, support local communities, and create a positive impact that ripples through your journey and beyond.

TWENTY-THREE
SUMMARY

Embarking on a journey as a mindful voyager entails a conscious effort to minimize our environmental impact, support local communities, and foster a deeper connection with the places we visit. Through the preceding chapters, we have explored various sustainable travel practices that empower us to explore the world responsibly and leave a positive legacy. In this summary, we will revisit the key principles and practices that define the mindful voyager's approach to travel.

The journey begins with packing light, embracing the art of minimalist travel. By prioritizing versatile clothing, choosing eco-conscious luggage, and minimizing waste, we reduce our footprint and create a more manageable and enjoyable travel experience. Choosing eco-conscious accommodations further amplifies our positive impact, as we support establishments that prioritize sustainable practices, conserve resources, and contribute to local economies.

Eating local is a culinary adventure that not only tantalizes our taste buds but also supports local communities and preserves cultural heritage. By seeking out fresh, seasonal ingredients from local farmers and producers, exploring local restaurants and eateries, and participating in cooking classes and food tours, we immerse ourselves in the flavors and traditions of a place. Slow travel, on the other hand, invites us to savor the journey, not just the destination. By choosing alternative modes of transportation, staying in locally owned accommodations, and engaging with local communities, we create more meaningful and immersive travel experiences.

Reducing waste is a fundamental principle of sustainable travel. By packing reusable alternatives, choosing accommodations that prioritize sustainability, and minimizing our consumption of single-use plastics, we can significantly reduce our environmental impact and contribute to a cleaner, healthier planet. Choosing low-impact transportation, such as walking, cycling, public transportation, trains, or electric vehicles, further reduces our carbon footprint and supports a more sustainable approach to travel.

Supporting local economies through purchasing from artisans and farmers is an act of reciprocity that empowers communities and preserves cultural heritage. By seeking out authentic products, understanding their stories, and appreciating their cultural significance, we contribute to the economic well-being of local artisans and farmers. Conserving water is a crucial aspect of sustainable travel, especially in water-scarce regions. By being mindful of our water usage, choosing accommodations that prioritize water conservation, and supporting local businesses that adopt water-saving practices, we can help protect this precious resource.

Reducing energy consumption is another key component of sustainable travel. By unplugging devices, conserving electricity and water, choosing energy-efficient accommodations, and supporting renewable energy initiatives, we can minimize our environmental impact and contribute to a cleaner energy future. Respecting wildlife and ecosystems is essential for preserving the natural world. By observing from a distance, following Leave No

Trace principles, and supporting conservation efforts, we can ensure that our presence in nature does not disrupt or harm these delicate systems.

Carbon offsetting provides a way to balance our environmental impact by investing in projects that reduce or remove greenhouse gases from the atmosphere. By choosing reputable providers and supporting verified projects, we can take responsibility for our carbon emissions and contribute to the global effort to combat climate change. Educating ourselves about our destination's culture and environment is a transformative act that enhances our appreciation, fosters cultural sensitivity, and promotes responsible tourism. By learning about the history, traditions, language, art, music, cuisine, and environment of a place, we open ourselves up to new perspectives and deepen our connection with the world.

Volunteering and giving back are integral aspects of sustainable tourism, enriching our travel experiences while leaving a positive legacy in the places we visit. By contributing our time, skills, and resources to local communities, we can create a lasting impact that extends far beyond our individual journeys. Leaving no trace is a philosophy that guides us to minimize our impact on natural environments. By following the principles of Leave No Trace, we can protect biodiversity, conserve resources, and ensure that future generations can enjoy the same pristine wilderness that we have been fortunate enough to experience.

Traveling by foot or bike offers a unique opportunity to explore the world at a slower pace, fostering a deeper connection with our surroundings and promoting a more sustainable and healthy way to travel. Avoiding single-use plastics and choosing reusable alternatives is a simple yet impactful way to reduce our environmental footprint and contribute to a cleaner planet. Shopping responsibly involves choosing souvenirs that do not harm the environment, exploit local artisans, or perpetuate unsustainable practices. By researching the origins of products, supporting local artisans and businesses, and choosing sustainable materials, we can ensure that our purchases have a positive impact.

Choosing sustainable tour operators involves researching their practices and certifications to ensure that they prioritize environmental protection, social responsibility, and economic empowerment. By supporting these companies, we contribute to a more ethical and sustainable tourism industry. Reflecting on our impact as travelers is a continuous journey of self-awareness, evaluation, and learning. By examining our choices and their consequences, we can identify areas for improvement, adopt more sustainable practices, and create a more positive legacy in the places we visit.

Creating a sustainable travel plan involves mindful decision-making throughout the entire process, from choosing destinations and transportation to accommodations and activities. By prioritizing sustainability in our planning, we can minimize our environmental impact, support local communities, and create a more enriching and responsible travel experience. In the end, the journey towards sustainable travel is a personal one, a continuous process of learning, growth, and transformation. By embracing these principles and practices, we not only minimize our negative impact but also create a positive ripple effect that can inspire others and contribute to a more sustainable future for tourism. As we embark on our future adventures, let us remember that we are not just travelers; we are stewards of the planet, responsible for protecting its beauty and diversity for generations to come.

ᗐᗐᗐ

Citation And References

This book represents the culmination of extensive research and meticulous analysis, incorporating a diverse range of sources, including numerous books, scholarly studies, and personal experiences. Additionally, I have scoured various websites to gather relevant information and data essential for the compilation of this work. I have taken every precaution to ensure the accuracy of the information presented and have diligently cited all sources to acknowledge their contributions.

Despite these efforts, the possibility of inadvertent errors remains. I deeply value the insights of my readers and appreciate any feedback that can help identify and rectify such inaccuracies. I encourage you to bring any discrepancies to my attention.

Your feedback is not only welcome but crucial, as it will aid in correcting current editions and enhancing the content of future ones. I am committed to maintaining the highest standards of accuracy and reliability in my work and thank you for your support and understanding.

Additionally, I firmly uphold the principle of freedom of speech and expression as guaranteed under Article 19(1)(a) of the Constitution of India, and I respect the diverse viewpoints and expressions of all readers.

ppp

Other Books Of The Author

1. Empowering Minds: A Journey into Women's Self-Discovery and Power
2. The Dynamics of Motivation: Catalyzing Thought into Action
3. Meditation and Mental Well Being: The Path to Inner Peace and Clarity
4. The Psychology of Child Education: Nurturing Future Generations
5. Ethical Enlightenment: A Modern Guide to Living with Integrity
6. Voices of Empowerment: Stories of Women Rising Against Odds
7. Social Psychology in Everyday Life: Understanding Human Connections
8. The Essence of Motivational Speaking: Inspiring Change in Others
9. Balancing Acts: Women, Work, and the Will to Lead
10. Guiding with Grace: Raising Children with Compassion and Awareness
11. The Power of Positive Aging: Embracing Life After Fifty
12. Building Resilient Communities: Social Work in Action
13. The Ethical Educator: Principles for Teaching and Learning
14. From Insight to Impact: Social Psychology for a Better World
15. The Ethics of Empathy: A Guide to Ethical Living
16. The Science of Empowering the Self: Navigating Life's Challenges with Psychological Wisdom
17. The Mindful Conscious Leader: Meditation Techniques for Modern Management
18. Pioneering Spirit: Women's Pathways to Leadership and Empowerment
19. Feeling to Healing: The Role of Emotional Intelligence in Child Development
20. Transformative Talks and Words of Inspiration: Insights into Motivational Oratory

21. Green Ethics: A Path to Sustainable Living
22. Spiritual Integrity: Navigating Life with Moral Compassion
23. Clean Living, Clean Society: The Ethics of Cleanliness
24. Patriotic Spirits: Building a Nation on Positive Attitudes
25. Innovative Integrity & Vibrant Visions: The Ethical and Entrepreneurial Spirit of Gujarat
26. Youthful Visions, Endless Possibilities: Inspiring Ethics and Motivation in Children
27. Living Your Legacy: How to Motivate Others by Living Your Values
28. Secret of Healing Conversations: Ethical Practices in Counselling and Therapy
29. Creative Kindness: Crafting a Life of Compassion and Creativity
30. The Power of Appreciation: How Gratitude Can Transform Your Relationships
31. Bhagavad-Gita: Messages
32. Science of Art: The New Frontier of Fashion Modernism
33. Vivekananda's Virtues: A Blueprint for Modern Living
34. Empower Her: Navigating the Path to Women's Entrepreneurship
35. The Boundless Classroom: Innovations in Global Education
36. The Language of Leadership: Communicating with Authenticity and Impact
37. The Warrior's Mantra: Deciphering the Hanuman Chalisa
38. Echoes of Empathy: Transformative Stories of Social Service
39. Artful Living: Cultivating Creativity in Your Daily Routine
40. Finding Your Why: Discovering Your Passions and Charting Your Course
41. The Role of Social Media in Shaping Self-Esteem and Interpersonal Relationships among Adolescents
42. Karma's Tapestry: Weaving a Life of Selfless Service
43. Altruistic Alchemy: Transforming Lives Through Giving
44. The Blueprint of Pro-Activeness and Productivity: Crafting Habits for Success
45. The Simplicity with Grounded Wisdom: Embracing Authenticity

Bhajan

101. Pilgrimage of the Soul: Spiritual Journeys in India

ᐻᐻᐻ

● 145 ●

Contact

Dr. Minakshi Bansal
Social Activist
Ahmedabad, Gujarat, Bharat
minakshiindiag20@yahoo.com

▷▷▷

|| LOKAHA SAMASTHAHA SUKHINO BHAVANTU ||